Implementation of Educational Policies for Minority Language Pupils in England and the United States

Implementation of Educational Policies for Minority Language Pupils in England and the United States:
a comparative case study analysis

AMANDA KIBLER

Monographs in International Education
Series Editors: Colin Brock & Rosarii Griffin

SYMPOSIUM
BOOKS

Symposium Books
PO Box 204, Didcot, Oxford OX11 9ZQ, United Kingdom
the book publishing division of wwwords Ltd
www.symposium-books.co.uk

Published in the United Kingdom, 2005

ISBN 1 873927 15 0

Typeset by wwwords Ltd
Printed and bound in the United Kingdom by Cambridge University Press

Contents

Acknowledgements

The dissertation on which this book is based would not have been possible without the knowledge, cooperation, and support of many individuals. I would like to thank Professor David Phillips for his excellent guidance and supervision throughout this project. Special appreciation is also due to all of the participants in my case studies who generously gave of their time and expertise to assist me: administrators, teachers, pupils, and especially R.P. and L.G., who were vital in arranging these visits. Finally, many thanks to Jeremy, for his patience and encouragement throughout this time.

Amanda Kibler

CHAPTER ONE

Introduction

As non-native English speakers make up a growing percentage of pupils in English and American schools, educational policies addressing English-language learning are becoming increasingly significant. Popular and governmental beliefs regarding the education of these pupils have resulted in *de facto* language policies which largely reflect political, rather than linguistic, realities. While research into second language acquisition has been prolific, these concerns seem to be placed well outside of current debates, as noted by Paulston:

> It is naïve to think that educational language policies ... are
> based on criteria that reasonably follow from research on
> developing bilingual proficiency; decisions are made primarily
> on political and economic grounds and reflect the values of
> those who have the power to make them. (1990, p. 187)

In such a situation, it is vital to analyse the development of these policies and their implementation at the school level.

The educational language policies of England and the United States generally view bilingualism in a 'subtractive' rather than in an 'additive' sense: the first language is seen as a factor which hampers pupils' success in mainstream education. While policy rhetoric may support the notion that a pupil's first language is a linguistic and cultural resource, literacy in this language is valued principally as a vehicle for learning English.

Such generalizations, however, ignore the range of language policy variations within the two countries. Case studies of two primary schools, one in England and one in the United States, were undertaken during the 2002-03 academic year. They help to illuminate how teachers and schools serving highly diverse linguistic and ethnic populations function within broader language policy directives. Special attention is given to teachers' and administrators' perceptions of the factors that hamper or facilitate the implementation of these initiatives.

This book attempts to address the following questions through a multi-level study, drawing upon information obtained through document analysis, staff interviews, and classroom observations:

1. How do language policies and their implementation relate to education?
2. How have the language-in-education policies of England and the United States developed, and how do they affect educational provision?
3. How are the following aspects of language policy for non-native English speakers implemented at the primary school level in England and the United States?

   - English-language literacy and development
   - First-language literacy and development
   - Pupil assessment

4. What factors affect language policy implementation at the primary school level?

The first research question is addressed in Chapter Two, which investigates the nature of language-in-education planning and policies and the issues involved in their interpretation. Additionally, Chapter Three analyses policies for minority language pupils in England and the United States and the statutory basis of educational provision. Chapter Four presents the methodology employed in this research; the comparative nature of the study and the use of a qualitative, case-study approach are explained in detail. Findings from the case studies, addressing research questions three and four, are presented in Chapters Five and Six. These analyses investigate the issues of policy implementation at a multi-lingual urban primary school in England and at a predominantly Spanish-speaking urban elementary school in the United States. Chapter Seven presents the findings of the case studies in a comparative context, drawing upon theory and empirical evidence to examine the manner in which internal, social, and political pressures affect policy implementation. Such an investigation can help expose underlying concerns at the school level resulting from language policies which dictate educational provision for increasingly diverse populations.

CHAPTER TWO

Language Planning and Policy in Education

1. Language Planning: a theoretical framework

The term *language planning*, first employed by Haugen in 1959, generally refers to 'deliberate efforts to influence the behaviour of others with respect to the acquisition, structure, or functional allocation of their language codes' (Cooper, 1989, p. 45). These efforts to influence language are undertaken by a variety of actors – from governments to schools to communities – to promote their agendas officially or informally. The relationship between majority and minority language speakers, along with a variety of other social factors, complicates the planning and policy development processes considerably.

Language planning encompasses a wide variety of activities but most often influences the status, corpus or acquisition of a language. Heinz Kloss first made the status versus corpus distinction, in which status planning involves efforts to change the realms in which a language is used, and corpus planning relates to changes in the form or structure of a language itself (Hornberger, 1994). Later, Cooper added acquisition planning, which focuses on organized efforts to learn a language (1989, p. 157).

Hornberger (1994) provides a useful framework that integrates the variety of language planning activities and goals (see Figure 1). She draws upon the work of both Haugen and Cooper to divide aspects of status, corpus, and acquisition planning into two areas: policy planning, focusing on language form; and cultivation planning, focusing on the function of languages.

The effects of language planning, especially in status and acquisition planning, can be analysed in their impact, or intended impact, on minority language speakers. Issues of status planning are significant because decisions about which languages are chosen as the standard, official, and national varieties implicitly exclude individuals who do not share this language or dialect. Also, such decisions influence whether a minority language is maintained or revived by altering the number of realms – governmental, social, and/or economic – in which the language is used. It is noteworthy, however, that formal proclamations regarding the status of a language do not always translate in practice, and that other planning measures may assign a language *de facto* status.

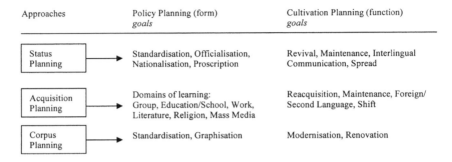

Figure 1. Language planning goals: an integrative framework (adapted from Hornberger, 1994, p. 78).

Acquisition planning applies to minority language communities, in that planning decisions can determine the realms in which a language can be learned. Although schools exist as only one of six domains in Hornberger's framework, education is widely regarded as a fundamental tool in language planning and policy implementation. The intended roles languages are meant to play in a community are largely dictated by the purposes for which they are acquired. Cooper (1989) classifies the overt goals of acquisition planning as reacquisition of a vernacular language, language maintenance, and learning a foreign or second language. Through these acquisition activities, speakers' dominant language may shift from one language to another.

Language planning, however, is not merely an organized pursuit of solutions to language problems (Corson, 1990); social factors also influence decisions. These broader social issues are recognized when language planning is positioned within a multi-disciplinary study known as the 'sociology of language' (Fishman, 1972). Indeed, Paulston notes that most language planning problems are socio-political in nature, and linguistic and psycho-educational factors are rarely the primary focus (Cummins, 2001a). Additionally, the individual identities of language speakers are complex and defy simple classifications. Drawing upon Hall's analysis of black cultural politics (1988), Leung et al (1997) suggest that:

> members of minority groups are not simple inheritors of fixed
> identities, ethnicities, cultures, and languages but are instead
> engaged in a continual collective and individual process of

making, remaking and negotiating these elements, thereby
constantly constructing dynamic new ethnicities. (p. 547)

These 'dynamic ethnicities' demand a re-evaluation of linguistic
repertoires on an individual basis. A person's linguistic identity can
therefore only be determined by looking at his or her levels of language
expertise, voluntary language affiliation, and inherited language
traditions (Rampton, 1990). In relating individual to group identities and
in analysing language planning, an awareness of the relationships
between language and society in political, social, and educational realms
is paramount.

Ruiz (1990) is widely cited for his typology of language
orientations. He believes that 'language planning and policy proceed
within one or more orientations, which are defined as a complex of
dispositions toward language and its role, and toward languages and
their role in society' (pp. 16-17). The following are descriptions of each
of his three orientations:

1. *Language-as-problem* – 'construes the targets of language policy
   to be a kind of social problem to be identified, eradicated,
   alleviated, or in some other way resolved.' The minority
   language (or 'local vernacular') is associated with poverty and
   disadvantage; alleviating these problems requires the
   replacement of the minority language with the dominant
   standard language. Subtractive bilingualism is viewed as a
   vehicle for achieving equality of opportunity.
2. *Language-as-right* – is often a reaction to *language-as-problem*
   policies. 'It confronts the assimilationist tendencies of dominant
   communities with arguments about the legal, moral, and natural
   right to local identity and language.' It rejects the idea that
   minority language communities are made 'better' when they lose
   their language and culture.
3. *Language-as-resource* – recognizes languages as social resources.
   'Policy statements formulated in this orientation should serve as
   guides by which language is preserved, managed, and
   developed.' These policies can reduce social conflict if they
   recognize the 'social importance of all communities and their
   languages' and if they '[promote] tolerance and even acceptance
   of minority languages'. (p. 17)

Similarly, Kloss (1971) explains that planning orientations underlie
international laws regarding minority languages and education. These
laws are either tolerance-oriented, resulting from a belief in 'language as
a right', or promotion-oriented, drawing upon the idea of 'language as a
resource'. Such linguistic values influence decisions determining the
functional use of a language in society, as well as the manner in which it
can be acquired and maintained.

2. Language Policy

A useful method of moving between theoretical and pragmatic concerns in this field is to consider the definition of 'language policy' in relation to 'language planning'. Some consider the two as distinct in purpose and product. For example, Kaplan & Baldauf (1997) consider language planning to be 'an activity ... intended to promote systematic linguistic change in some community of speakers', whereas language policy is the 'body of ideas, laws, regulations, rules and practices intended to achieve the planned language change in the society' (p. xi). For the purposes of this study, Ricento's explanation appears to be most useful:

> I deliberately use 'language policy' as a superordinate term
> which subsumes 'language planning.' Language policy [and
> its] research [are] not only concerned with official and
> unofficial acts of governmental and other institutional entities,
> but also with the historical and cultural events and processes
> that have influenced, and continue to influence, societal
> attitudes and practices with regard to language use, acquisition
> and status. (2000, p. 23)

The theories of language planning, as discussed in the previous section, thereby act as useful typologies when considering the extra-linguistic forces at work in language-related policies. Issues of equality, integration, politics, and social power all affect language policy approaches, development, and implementation.

Several factors can determine the outcome of a given language policy. In *Motivation in Language Planning and Language Policy*, Ager (2001) concludes that decisions depend on the identity of the decision-makers, their motivations, their attitudes toward the languages in question, and the goals of the policy. As a result, simplistic models of language policy development and implementation have limited value. For example, Corson (1990) draws upon the work of Rubin (1977) and Horvath (1980) to present a four-step method for carrying out a language plan:

1. Fact-gathering: find out about needs of 'clients'
2. Decision-making: determine strategy, resource allocation, and set goals
3. Implementation: mobilize resources and coordinate activities
4. Evaluation: monitor and modify policy as needed.

Such a framework, however, does not recognize that many decisions are made without any consultation with the populations who will be affected; that the policy may be enacted without adequate strategic development; that implementation may be less than universal; or that the evaluation may not fully measure the policy's implications. Models such as these are helpful only if one considers the identities and socio-political status of the actors involved and the reasons why certain outcomes might occur.

In a more detailed characterization of language policy approaches, Schmidt (2000) classifies policies that vary in their promotion of linguistic and cultural status equality as well as their promotion of social integration for minority language groups (Figure 2).

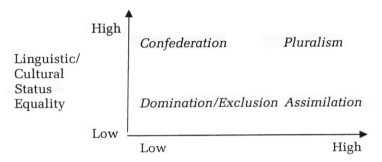

Figure 2. Typology of language policy approaches (adapted from Schmidt, 2000, p. 57).

In 'confederations', exemplified by such countries as Switzerland, Belgium, and India, languages are each given physical and/or functional areas of their own. In a 'pluralist' society, such as Canada, language policies try to 'bring all speakers together as member of the same nation while respecting native languages' (p. 57). 'Assimilationist' language policies, however, view bilingualism as a deficit, rather than a resource, and attempt to eliminate any potential linguistic conflict by encouraging a shift toward the dominant language through marginalizing the functional and social uses for the native language. Notably, many regard the language policies in the United States and England as assimilationist, both historically (Rassool, 1995; Ager, 1996; Gravelle, 1996; Thompson et al, 1996) and contemporarily (Stubbs, 1991; Rassool, 1995; Harris, 1997; Wiley, 2000). Finally, policy approaches with a goal of 'domination and exclusion' use the majority language as a tool to exclude others from participation in society. An extreme example of such an abuse of power is that of apartheid-era South Africa. While a nation's language approach may be grouped into one of these general categories, the purposes of specific policies may differ, and their application may vary over time and by location.

An analysis of language policies must acknowledge the political environment in which decisions are made. While policy development occurs at local and regional levels, the nation-state is most often a decisive factor in constructing an ideological language framework. While not all nations can be considered 'nationalistic', an overriding concern of many countries is unity: political, cultural, and linguistic. Associated with the rise of political nationalism is an 'emphasis on cultural and linguistic homogeneity' (May, 2001, p. 6). Therefore, many nation-state policies can be assumed to view language diversity as a problem, rather than a right or a resource. In E.D. Hirsch's influential book *Cultural Literacy: what every American needs to know* (1988), multi-lingualism and multi-culturalism are seen as a threat to a common set of cultural values for the country, thus undermining national unity (Cummins, 2001b). Coulmas (1998) even believes that 'the nation-state as it has evolved since the French Revolution is the natural enemy of minorities' (p. 67). Linguistic assimilation would seem to be the most expedient method of establishing the necessary national sense of unity, and education is seen as the primary means of achieving this: 'after all, education is recognized as a key institution – perhaps *the* key institution – in the apparatus of the modern nation-state' (May, 2001, p. 167).

Issues of social power may be even more significant than political factors in language policy development. Those who speak the standard version of the majority language have a distinct advantage; according to De Beaugrande, 'the elite can communicate and interact with the rest, but always from a position of superior power' (1999, p. 108). This perceived linguistic superiority can manifest itself in a refusal to cede this control to any other competing language groups. The result is often linguistic discrimination against minority language speakers, which Phillipson has called 'linguicism' (1992, p. 47). This linguicism is 'steadily assuming the functions of more conspicuous and discredited modes of discrimination, such as racism and ethnocentrism' (De Beaugrande, 1999, p. 108). Such attitudes can be revealed overtly, as in the case of English-education-only policies in Arizona, California, and Massachusetts in the United States, or more covertly, as in the case of the National Curriculum in England, by increasing pressure to learn and use 'standard English' in the classroom (see Appendix C).

Issues of policy, then, must be considered in their political, social, and linguistic contexts. De Beaugrande warns that policies' outward goals may in fact mask less altruistic aims:

> We must be objective in recognizing not just the diversity of languages and language varieties but also the deployment of that diversity to legitimize inequality and exclusion despite official theories of equality and inclusion. (1999, p. 110)

Thus, any language policy should be scrutinized carefully to determine its true intentions, implicit ideologies, and possible effects. An analysis of language-in-education policies is necessary, therefore, because educational systems often serve to implement these overt and covert policies within a society.

3. Language-in-Education Policies for Minority Language Speakers

In England and the United States, there are no governmentally-enunciated language policies, and so 'there is an implicit recognition that the way things are done is indeed a policy, in the absence of competing or consistently applied alternatives' (Herriman & Burnaby, 1996, p. 3). Education is one of the areas in which this *de facto* language policy is most visible. Often, however, when language policies are informal, the educational provision for linguistic minorities must 'often rely on local circumstances and micro-level policy rather than on any overall approach to the situation' (Ager, 1996, pp. 52-53.) The ambiguity of such language-in-education policies and approaches often makes it difficult to protect the rights of minority language speakers consistently (Stubbs, 1991). Local education authorities and schools are implicitly involved in *de facto* language policy situations. In the absence of any specified policy, local institutions are left to determine which language will be used as a medium of instruction and which language programmes will be established for linguistic majorities and minorities. Such decisions, again, are a product of social and political factors as well as linguistic concerns.

While education can be seen merely as a vehicle for language policy implementation, David Corson (1990) finds a broader goal for schools working with linguistic and ethnically diverse pupils:

> It is no longer enough in pluralist societies, where group and individual language rights are recognised, to base education exclusively on the standard language as used by dominant groups in society. Matters of social justice and equality coupled with an explosion of knowledge about linguistic issues and their effects on language development have made the language tasks of schools much more complex than they seemed to be in the past. (p. 20)

In addressing language policy issues, then, educational decision-makers must account for both the social context and the growing body of language acquisition research in determining sound language policies. Also, as schools struggle with the demands of multiple languages and ethnicities, the potential of schools to help or hinder 'social justice' should not be underestimated. Pupils from diverse linguistic and cultural backgrounds may also be the victims of discrimination within educational environments. August & Hakuta found that 'language-minority students may be treated differently from mainstream pupils as a result of forces both within and outside of school that implicitly and explicitly promote and sustain the perspectives and institutions of the majority' (1997, p. 152). Several studies assert that teachers may unknowingly perpetuate biases against pupils of other ethnic and linguistic backgrounds (Biggs & Edwards, 1991; Corson, 1991; Nyakatawa

15

& Siraj-Blatchford, 1994). Pupils may even be seen 'not as the principal victims of an education which has failed to cater to their needs, but as the primary cause of this failure' (Biggs & Edwards, 1991, p. 161). Therefore, educational systems and schools face a problem of linguistic and social re-acculturation themselves.

4. Language Acquisition Research and Language-in-Education Policies

Although policies for minority language pupils are not merely a linguistic concern, knowledge of language acquisition research is crucial in evaluating policy decisions. Policy may rarely reflect research results, but a variety of studies have provided guidance in some of the following questions addressed by language policies:

- How long does it take a student to learn the majority language in school?
- Which are the most effective methods for teaching the majority language?
- What is the role of the first language in acquiring another one?
- What are the most effective strategies for teaching the majority language in school?

The broad variety of possible language acquisition programmes and of the terminology employed in describing them means that research must be approached critically. For example, the lack of a strict definition of a 'bilingual programme' or an 'immersion programme' means that students in the same 'type' of educational programme may be receiving very different language input. Carefully constructed studies do, however, provide valuable insight into the language learning process.

Educational policies that address language learners are often concerned with the length of time for which language support should be provided. Thomas & Collier (2001), in their five-year study of over 210,000 students in the United States, found that English-language learners take at least four years to reach grade level performance in English, and then only if they have had at least four years of schooling in their own language. Students without first-language schooling are often never able to reach grade level performance. According to McLaughlin (1992), the oral language that students can acquire in two or three years may mask the fact that four to six years are necessary 'to acquire the level of proficiency for understanding language in its instructional uses' (p. 5). Thus, language learning is a gradual process in which students need long-term support.

Several theories seek to illuminate the relationship between first-language learning and subsequent language acquisition. Cummins & Swain's *Bilingualism in Education* (1986) proposes two such theories from which much subsequent work has been derived. Their linguistic interdependence hypothesis posits that all languages an individual may learn share a common underlying proficiency. Therefore, 'experience with either language can promote development of the proficiency underlying both languages' (p. 82). Additionally, Cummins & Swain, in their threshold hypothesis, contend that the development of the second language should not be introduced before a certain competence is achieved in the first language:

> There may be threshold levels of language competence which
> bilingual children must attain in their first language in order to
> avoid cognitive disadvantages and to allow the potentially
> beneficial aspects of becoming bilingual to influence cognitive
> functioning. (p. 6)

Therefore, a high level of second-language competence is dependent on a measure of first-language development.

Much research has also been conducted to discover the most effective manner of instruction for English-language learners. A multitude of pedagogical approaches operate in contemporary schools, but some of the most prominent in England and the United States include the following (for a complete classification, see Appendix A):

- Submersion (structured immersion, withdrawal classes, sheltered English)
- Transitional bilingual
- Maintenance/heritage language bilingual
- Two-way dual language. (Baker & Jones, 1998)

This list is not exhaustive, and each category can be further defined by whether the language is taught in isolation or through academic content. A wide variety of studies in the United States support the notion that programmes which focus on maintaining and developing competence in both languages to an advanced level result in higher achievement in the second language (Cummins & Swain, 1986; Ramirez et al., 1991; Thomas & Collier, 1997, 2001). In England, bilingual pilot projects have resulted in improved first language skills and improved, or at least unhindered, development in English (Corson, 1991, 1998; Gravelle, 1996). However, bilingual programs are a highly contentious issue: 'the question of how best to promote literacy learning in either or both languages is ... overshadowed by the politically more volatile issues of which language should be used and for how long' (Snow et al, 1998, p. 39).

Regardless of the exact title assigned to a specific language programme, many of the most effective incorporate bilingual assistance or instruction. Several 'predictors of success' relate to successful language acquisition. For example, Thomas & Collier (1997) have determined that the following variables are key predictors:

– Cognitively complex on-grade-level [age-appropriate] academic instruction through students' first language for as long as possible and cognitively complex on-grade-level [age-appropriate] academic instruction through the second language [English] for part of the school day,
– The use of current approaches to teaching the academic curriculum through two languages [such as thematic units involving interactive teaching and cooperative learning strategies], and
– A transformed sociocultural context for minority language pupils' schooling [in which bilingualism is enrichment rather than remedial assistance]. (Thomas & Collier, 1997, pp. 15-16)

Corson (1991) discusses findings from Lily Wong Fillmore's study 'Learning English through Bilingual Instruction' in the United States. She found the following four instructional factors to be significant in developing English academic language skills of Hispanic and Chinese minority language speakers:

- High-quality teaching
- High-quality instructional language
- Effective classroom management
- Provision of equal opportunities for the practice of English.

However, it must be noted that the student group in this study was not homogeneous; students learned language more effectively in different classroom environments. Indeed, Harris (1997) and Leung et al (1997) stress the need to view language learners individually, each with unique linguistic identities.

Each learner's language needs will therefore vary according to his or her cultural and academic background, individual ability, and personality. Thus, teachers and schools must employ a wide variety of language acquisition strategies to encourage learning. Some of the many strategies promoted in language acquisition research include active learning, peer interaction, collaboration, and group work (Nyakatawa & Siraj-Blatchford, 1994; Thomas & Collier, 1997; Putney & Wink, 1998; Texas Education Agency Program Evaluation Unit, 2000). Also, Cummins' theoretical framework of language proficiency, widely used in second language teacher training and curriculum guidance, suggests that students learn skills best when they are embedded in a comprehensible and meaningful communicative context (Cummins & Swain, 1986; Hall, 1995). Finally, a teaching strategy found to be useful, especially in structured immersion or sheltered English situations, is that of 'partnership teaching' (Gravelle, 1996) or 'co-teaching' (Wertheimer & Honingsfeld, 2000), in which mainstream classroom teachers and language specialist teachers jointly plan and teach classes that include language learners. While these strategies represent a minute proportion of those recommended by language acquisition research, they provide a useful guide in envisaging what a language policy should include or encourage.

5. Implementation of Policies for Minority Language Speakers

The actual implementation of language-in-education policies at the classroom, school, or district level can be affected by a variety of internal and external factors. In an investigation of multi-lingual primary and secondary schools in Amsterdam, Miedema (1997) found that these institutions faced several dilemmas in implementing their policies for minority language speakers. Classrooms were often provided with inappropriate and inadequate resources, as well as a curriculum which failed to incorporate language development into subjects such as mathematics or science. Difficulties at the school level included:

- external circumstances that placed limitations and demands on the schools' priorities,
- societal pressures, from back-to-basics movements to budget cuts, and a general lack of understanding of minorities' circumstances and needs, and
- pressure on schools to improve examination and assessment scores. (p. 58).

Further implementation issues are analysed in a study of California school districts by Cardinale et al (1999), before bilingual education was outlawed in the state (see Appendix I). In this study, districts encountered difficulties in implementing their minority language programmes due to problems in finding qualified bilingual teachers, in avoiding the 'ghettoization' effect of bilingual programmes, in negotiating political forces and racial relations, and in meeting logistical demands. Corson explains that minority language provision that incorporates, supports, or maintains pupils' first languages may be untenable if the diversity of languages spoken is too great (1991, p. 17). Regardless of the specific situation, however, in most educational systems, programmes designed to support minority language speakers must meet an increasing demand at a time when *all* sectors of educational systems are seen as meriting extra funding and resources.

CHAPTER THREE

Language-in-Education Policies in England and the United States

To provide a historical, political, and social context for the case studies in Chapters Five and Six, this chapter outlines the general features of language-in-education policies at the time the case study research was undertaken.

1. England's Policies for Minority Language Pupils

While pupils learning English as a non-native language are referred to as 'limited English proficient' (LEP) in the United States, these same individuals are labeled 'bilingual' or 'English as an additional language' (EAL) in England. To avoid confusion with the 'bilingual' education programmes in the United States, those individuals in England whose first language is not English and who are acquiring the language in school will be referred to as EAL pupils.

The EAL student population in England is proportionately similar to that of LEP students in the United States. One must approach these statistics with caution, however; there are significant regional and national variations in how EAL or LEP students are identified and how their fluency in English is assessed. According to the then Department for Education and Employment's *Statistical First Release* (DfEE, 1999a), EAL students represent 8.1% of the compulsory school population in England. No systematic longitudinal data are available, however, to account for the growth of the EAL population in relation to the total school population. In analyzing the lack of specific EAL data, Leung (2001) notes that, 'To this day detailed figures are conspicuous by their absence' (p. 162).

While the DfEE's data do not classify EAL students by their native language, information is available on the ethnic identities of the overall student population. 'Non-white' students in England comprise approximately 11.65% of the school population, including 1.5% Black Caribbean, 1.1% Black African, 0.8% Black 'Other', 2.5% Indian, 2.55% Pakistani, 0.95% Bangladeshi, 0.35% Chinese, and 1.95% 'Other'.

When the first significant influxes of minority language pupils occurred in the late 1950s and 1960s, EAL provision in England was predominantly the result of local governments' response to this 'rapidly emerging need', rather than a 'planned national development based on anticipation' (Leung, 2001, p. 155). While major national education legislation remains relatively silent on the issue of EAL education, increasing guidance has been provided through the Department of Education, the national inspectorate (OFSTED), the Qualifications and Curriculum Authority (QCA) and its predecessors, and a number of quasi-governmental and private organizations.

A series of governmental circulars and reports have provided general advice to local education authorities (LEAs). The LEAs had, until the mid-1960s, been developing their own EAL programs with only minimal advice from the Ministry, which has been successively known as the Department for Education and Science (DES), the Department for Education (DFE), the Department for Education and Employment (DfEE), and the Department for Education and Skills (DfES). Significant among these documents is the Bullock Report (1975), which advocated an awareness and appreciation of linguistic diversity in schools (Ager, 1996). The Bullock Report recommended integrating pupils into mainstream provision, rather than educating them in separate language centers (DES, 1975).

The Swann Report (1985) further emphasized this point, by strongly discouraging not only the use of separate language centres, but even the withdrawal of EAL pupils from mainstream classrooms. Withdrawal, the Swann Report stated, impoverished both curricular access and social learning. Competence in English, rather than first languages, was emphasized: 'English language is a central unifying factor in "being British" and is key to participation on equal terms as a full member of this society' (Committee of Inquiry into the Education of Children from Ethnic Minority Groups, 1985, p. 385). 'Mother tongue' maintenance was found to be the community's, rather than the school's, responsibility.

The use of first languages in schools, however, has more recently been encouraged as a means of accessing the curriculum for EAL pupils. For example, in *The National Literacy Strategy: supporting pupils learning English as an additional language* (2002), the DfES suggests that bilingual and multi-lingual teaching assistants should use EAL pupils' first languages for:

- explaining instructions, tasks, and curriculum content,
- redefining words and phrases critical to a child's understanding,
- encouraging children to articulate ideas in their preferred language,
- developing children's confidence in expressing themselves in English,

  – presenting themselves ... as role models, and
  – promoting home-school liaison. (p. 45)

The National Curriculum and standards for pupils of compulsory school age were first established through the 1988 Education Reform Act, which transformed educational provision in England (Holdaway, 1991). The Cox Report (DES, 1989), designed to suggest the scope and standards for the subject of English within the National Curriculum, established that English was to be the only medium of instruction in schools; pupils could not study *in* their first languages, but they could study them as discrete subjects – 'foreign' languages (Stubbs, 1991). There are no separate EAL content standards, but objectives regarding all pupils' use of 'Standard English' in speaking, listening, reading, and writing are included in the English curriculum (see Appendix C).

As part of 'Principles for Inclusion' in *English: The National Curriculum for England (program of study),* the following is suggested regarding 'pupils who are learning English as an additional language':

  – Pupils for whom English is an additional language have
  diverse needs ...
  – Planning should take account of such factors as the pupil's
  age, length of time in this country, previous education
  experience and skills in other languages ...
  – Teachers should plan learning opportunities to help pupils
  develop their English and should aim to provide the support
  pupils need to take part in all subject areas.
  – Teachers should take specific action to help pupils who are
  learning English as an additional language by:
    – developing their spoken and written English, [and]
    – ensuring access to the curriculum and to assessment.
  (DfEE, 1999b, p. 49)

The National Curriculum's *Handbook for Primary Teachers in England* also addresses cultural development as an aim in 'Learning across the National Curriculum':

  Pupils' cultural development involves pupils acquiring an
  understanding of cultural traditions and an ability to
  appreciate and respond to a variety of aesthetic experiences.
  They acquire a respect for their own cultures and that of others
  ... (QCA, 1999)

Although these and other suggestions were considered inadequate by many advocates for EAL students, including NALDIC (the National Association for Language Development in the Curriculum), they remain the primary guidance for teachers on EAL issues in the English National Curriculum (Gravelle, 1996).

While not specifically included in the National Curriculum, the National Literacy and Numeracy Strategies (NLS and NNS), introduced in 1998, are also significant aspects of the statutory curriculum in England. The literacy strategy, delivered through a daily Literacy Hour, comprises the bulk of targeted English-language learning opportunities within the curriculum at the primary level and therefore merits specific investigation in the EAL context (for more information on the NLS, see Appendix D). There is no separate provision for EAL pupils within the literacy strategy, because, as the Department for Education and Employment claims, 'The NLS Framework and the Literacy Hour are appropriate for children who speak English as an Additional Language ... The National Literacy Strategy [is] perfectly consistent with teaching children who speak English as an Additional Language' (DfEE, 1998a, p. 77). Subsequently, the DfEE (1998b), DfES (2002) and NALDIC (1998) have produced training materials and discussion documents which address how to adequately provide for EAL pupils' needs in the Literacy Hour. An OFSTED analysis of the NLS during 1998-2002 reports, however, that 'many schools do not make any specific provision and have no formal policy for their [EAL learners'] support' (OFSTED, 2002, p. 25).

Assessment of EAL pupils is undertaken within the context of school-wide as well as EAL-specific measures. All English-language learners are required to participate in National Curriculum assessments, although some new arrivals may be exempted, and pupils may qualify for first-language interpretation for some of the examinations (for a description of the ages at which certain subjects are assessed, see Appendix B). The Qualifications and Curriculum Authority provided the first national framework for EAL-specific assessment, entitled *A Language in Common: assessing English as an additional language* (QCA, 2000). In this framework, assessment scales relate 'steps' of achievement to National Curriculum levels for reading, writing, and listening/speaking. Additionally, the Northern Association of Support Services for Equality and Achievement (NASSEA), an organization of Ethnic Minority Achievement Service (EMAS) teams, developed and published a modified version of this scale, which has been implemented in a number of LEAs.

Since 1998, funding to support EAL pupils has been provided primarily by the Ethnic Minority Achievement Grant, issued by the Department for Education and Skills, although local authorities and schools may supplement this amount. The grant's objectives focus on *all* ethnic minorities, rather than only those who speak English as an additional language:

> The Ethnic Minority Achievement grant is intended to provide equality of opportunity for all minority ethnic groups. In particular:

a. to meet the particular needs of pupils for whom English is an additional language (EAL), and

b. to raise standards of achievement for those minority ethnic groups who are particularly at risk of under-achieving. (DfEE, 1998c)

Once the grant is transferred to LEAs, 85% of the total funding must be devolved to schools so that they can 'determine their own priorities' (DfES, 2003a). The grant does not stipulate how schools should use this funding, and so they have discretion in how the objectives stated above are fulfilled, through staffing, training, or other initiatives devised to address EAL needs and raise ethnic minority achievement.

Because of this flexibility in policy, EAL classroom support and staffing can vary widely. Unlike provision in the United States, in-class support of EAL pupils is not a 'statutory obligation' of the school or the local education authority (Leung, 2001, p. 166). Although private organizations offer certificates or advanced degrees in EAL and related fields, EAL specialist teachers are not generally required to have such a qualification, either at the primary or secondary level. Although all teacher training institutions differ in their curricular arrangements, the Teacher Training Agency's (TTA) requirements for qualified teacher status do not require that prospective teachers have a knowledge of EAL issues or strategies. Additionally, EAL is not offered as a secondary level 'specialist subject' like English, Mathematics, Science, or other fields. The TTA has, however, published guidance for how initial teacher training providers '*might* plan opportunities for trainees to examine and develop their understanding [of EAL issues]' [my emphasis] (TTA, 2000, p. 45).

EAL provision in England's maintained schools can be described as a 'diffused curriculum concern' (Leung, 2001), in which pupils' language needs are met within the mainstream classroom largely through the assistance of EAL specialist teachers and/or other language support. Although national mandates and legislation regarding EAL policy are limited, the Department of Education and other organizations have offered local authorities and schools general 'guidance', which has then been translated into more specific LEA and school practices and procedures.

2. The United States' Policies for Minority Language Pupils

The overall responsibility for education in the United States rests primarily with the individual states, as established in the Constitution of 1789. The federal government has influenced education, however, through congressional legislation and Supreme Court judicial rulings. With regard to the education of minority language pupils, state and local authorities must fulfill these federal requirements but are allowed broad powers of interpretation. Language policies have gained importance in the United States largely because of the growing population of non-native English-speaking pupils categorized as 'limited English proficient' (LEP). The term 'limited' undoubtedly has negative connotations, but it remains the most common descriptive term in US policies which refer to non-native speakers still in the process of acquiring English fluency. In 2000-2001, LEP students comprised almost 9.8% of the compulsory school population in the United States, a proportion which had grown by 95% since 1991 (National Center for Educational Statistics, 2002). Students with Spanish as a first language represent 76.6% of this total, while speakers of Vietnamese, Hmong, Creole/Haitian, Korean, Cantonese and over twenty-nine other languages account for the remaining LEP students (Kindler, 2002).

The use of first languages in American schooling, however, is not a recent development. Although no federal mandate existed, 'bilingual and vernacular education were widely, if inconsistently, available' from the colonial era until the early 1900s. As Crawford (2000) explains, however, wartime fears contributed to a growing desire to 'Americanize the Immigrant,' which led to the virtual disappearance of first-language instruction in the years preceding World War I (p. 100). From then until the 1960s, education for linguistic minorities largely consisted of English immersion or 'sink-or-swim' strategies, with few remedial services provided (National Center for English Language Acquisition, 2002a). While space does not permit an exhaustive investigation of federal legislative and judicial decisions affecting these pupils since the early twentieth century, some of the most salient are explained below.

The federal government first intervened in language-in-education policies in 1968, when Congress unanimously passed the Bilingual Education Act (Title VII of the Elementary and Secondary Education Act). This legislation established a mandate for the bilingual education of economically disadvantaged minority language pupils (NCELA, 2002a), but did not specify a pedagogical approach for doing so. Because the measure passed with broad support but little funding, it was seen as symbolic rather than substantive (Schmidt, 2000). Later reauthorizations of and amendments to this act have appeared to support English-only language development programmes or transitional (early-exit) bilingual programs, which receive the majority of funding allocations (Carrasquillo & Rodriguez, 2001). *No Child Left Behind* (United States Department of Education, 2001), the most recent reauthorization of the Elementary and Secondary Education Act, replaced the Bilingual Education Act's Title VII provisions with its own Title III objectives, which focus on promoting English acquisition and meeting curriculum content standards. Although Title III does not proscribe bilingual education programs, Crawford (2002) views this most recent legislation as a dramatic shift in language policy, from an approach that supported first language teaching to one in which '[only] one thing is [now] certain: the rapid teaching of English will take precedence at every turn'. The impact of this recent national legislation, with its increasing focus on the development of skills in English rather than in pupils' first languages, will undoubtedly affect the manner in which states address LEP pupils' needs.

The Supreme Court decision which most profoundly affected current language-in-education policies is the *Lau v. Nichols* decision of 1974. In the 1960s and 1970s, many school districts had been slow to implement the Bilingual Education Act or the Civil Rights Act of 1964, which prohibited the exclusion of individuals from federal programme participation on the basis of race, colour, or national origin (Crawford, 2000; NCELA, 2002a). As a result, pupils with few or no English skills were still being taught in the same manner as native English speakers. In *Lau v. Nichols*, the court ruled that this 'identical' treatment was not sufficient, and schools must provide appropriate language support to ensure pupils equal access to the curriculum, because in the current situation, 'students who [did] not understand English [were] effectively foreclosed from any meaningful education' (Crawford, 2000, p. 92). However, the court decision did not mandate any single pedagogical approach to teaching non-native English speakers. A later Supreme Court ruling, *Plyler v. Doe* (1982), declared that the children of illegal immigrants must have equal access to public schools, thereby ensuring that all pupils would have protection under the *Lau v. Nichols* decision (Texas Education Agency, 1998). The Office of Civil Rights has played a significant role in monitoring states', districts', and schools' compliance with the *Lau* decision (Ricento, 1996).

The overall lack of a specific pedagogical mandate in language-in-education policies has resulted in a federal structure that is largely advisory in nature. The US Department of Education conducts research, provides policy consultation, and issues grants through the Office for English Language Acquisition, Enhancement, and Academic Achievement for Limited English Proficient Students (OELA). This office administers the National Clearinghouse for English Language Acquisition and Language Instruction Educational Programs, which 'collect[s], analyze[s], and disseminate[s] information relating to the effective education of linguistically and culturally diverse learners in the US' (NCELA, 2002b).

Provision for LEP pupils varies greatly from state to state. For example, twenty-three states have a teaching specialization in English as a second language (ESL) and/or bilingual education, and forty-three states have legislative provision for LEP programs (NCELA, 1999, 2002c). Although the Department of Education has not produced any ESL or bilingual content standards, the TESOL (Teachers of English to Speakers of Other Languages) organization has developed basic ESL standards for pre-kindergarten through twelfth-grade pupils. This conceptual framework has been designed to 'address the questions of what students should know as a result of their ESL instruction' (TESOL, 1997). Individual states have been encouraged to develop and align their own ESL standards to those developed by TESOL.

To gain insight into the implementation of language-in-education policy in the US, it is necessary to focus on a single state's provision and interpretation of federal guidelines for minority language pupils. Texas, one of seven states with over 100,000 LEP pupils, has developed a comprehensive legislative and curricular framework for ESL and bilingual education. Out of 4,071,433 students of compulsory school age in 2000-2001, 570,603 (14%) were designated as LEP (NCES, 2002). Spanish is the dominant first language of these students; Spanish speakers comprise 94% of the LEP population in Texas, while Vietnamese and Cantonese represent 2% and 1% respectively (Kindler, 2002).

State legislation which addresses minority language pupils is found in the Texas Education Code (TEC), and specific guidelines pertaining to the implementation of the TEC are included in the Texas Administrative Code (TAC). The *Commissioner's Rules Concerning State [sic] Plan for Educating Limited English Proficient Students* outline state policy which aims to 'ensure equal educational opportunity' (TAC, 2002, 89.1201). Variations of this statute have been in place since the Texas Bilingual Education and Training Act of 1973 (San Miguel, 1987). The *Commissioner's Rules* state that each school district shall:

> 1. identify limited English proficient students based on criteria established by the state [through approved language assessment tests in English and, if possible, in their first language],
> 2. provide bilingual education and English as a second language programs, as integral parts of the regular program ...,
> 3. seek certified teaching personnel [in ESL or bilingual education], and
> 4. assess achievement for essential skills and knowledge [mainstream curriculum] to ensure accountability for limited English proficient students and schools that serve them. (TAC, 2002, 89.1201)

For any school district with an enrollment of twenty or more LEP pupils in any single language classification at the same grade level, the district must offer a bilingual programme in the elementary grades, a bilingual or ESL programme at the middle-school level, and an ESL programme at the high-school level (for grade level designations for elementary, middle, and high school, see Appendix J). Districts may concentrate bilingual or ESL programmes at a limited number of campuses, as long as the overall population of the school does not include more than 60% limited English proficient pupils (TAC, 2002, 89.1235).

The amount of bilingual and/or ESL instruction pupils receive should be 'commensurate with the students' level of proficiency', and the Texas Education Agency is charged with developing guidelines for these programs (TAC, 2002, 89.1205). Although the TAC does not specify methodological approaches, it does mandate that the bilingual education programme 'shall be a full-time program of instruction in which both the students' home language and English shall be used for instruction' in literacy, mathematics, science, health and social studies (89.1205). Additionally, ESL approaches 'shall be intensive programs of instruction designed to develop proficiency in the comprehension, speaking, reading, and composition in the English language' through literacy instruction and through 'second language methods' in the content areas (89.1205). For both bilingual and ESL programmes, districts must use state-adopted instructional and supplementary materials.

A Language Proficiency Assessment Committee (LPAC), established at the school or district level and consisting of a combination of teachers and parents, determines pupils' eligibility for enrollment in and exit from the bilingual or ESL programme, as well as participation in state assessments (TAC, 2002, 89.1220). (For a description of the ages at which certain subjects are assessed, see Appendix J.) Depending on the length of time pupils have been enrolled in US schools, their grade level, and their proficiency in their first language and/or English, they may take the English or Spanish versions of the state assessment tests, or may be exempted from the tests entirely for a limited number of years. LEP pupils' English-language development is also assessed annually through state-approved oral and/or reading proficiency tests (TAC, 2001).

The Texas Administrative Code also includes state curriculum standards – the Texas Essential Knowledge and Skills – for each academic subject at each grade level. Spanish language arts standards and English as a second language standards, developed in 1991, are outlined as distinct areas of the state curriculum (TEA, 1998). These standards are identical to those for the mainstream English language arts curriculum but include additional provisions for each objective to reflect minority language pupils' development in Spanish and/or English (TAC, 1998).

Through legislative policy, the establishment of curricular standards, and the availability of an ESL/bilingual teaching qualification, the language acquisition of LEP pupils has developed as a distinct educational discipline. State policies and standards, combined with federal mandates regarding the education of minority language pupils, place a responsibility on districts and local schools to provide equal access and opportunity for LEP pupils either through first-language or developmentally appropriate English-language instruction.

CHAPTER FOUR

Methodology

1. Comparative Education Aims

As a result of an increasingly mobile global population, minority and majority language issues in education are prominent worldwide. Countries differ greatly in their linguistic identities, and their language policy goals and implementation reflect several approaches to language-in-education. In such a situation, comparative methods are especially valuable. As Harold Noah states:

> The fundamental assertion of comparative study is that we can
> truly comprehend ourselves in the context of a secure
> knowledge of other societies: knowledge that is parochial is
> partial, in both senses of that word, and therefore potentially
> dangerous. It is knowledge without completeness, and it is
> knowledge without appreciation of the rest of the world's
> experience. (1986, pp. 164-165)

Thus, a thorough understanding of an educational system's policies for non-native English speakers requires study of other systems, to 'see various practices and procedures in a very wide context that helps to throw light upon them' (Phillips, 1999, p. 16). This broad perspective is an essential component in comparative approaches, recognizing the effects of cultural, social, political, geographical, and economic factors that have shaped and continue to influence educational systems. Careful study of contextual factors can therefore prevent superficial comparisons and simplistic analyses of language-in-education policies.

The recognition of context complicates research, in both the breadth and sophistication of information that must be compiled to reach an accurate analysis of an educational situation. The slection of an appropriate methodological framework, therefore, is paramount. George Bereday's often-cited 'stages of comparative methodology' (1964) offer a clear starting point in organizing comparative study, dividing research into four phases: description, interpretation, juxtaposition, and comparison. Bereday's stress on thorough and systematic data-gathering and description, as well as a subsequent analysis of these data in the light of historical, geographical, social, and economic factors (interpretation), should underlie any comparative research effort. However, a combination of these first two stages might be a more realistic approach; the application of context in the second stage implies that context can, in fact, be separated from the educational situation under study. Language-in-education policies and practice are securely embedded in political and social issues, and so this study attempts to gather and represent data holistically, without artificially separating any 'pure' pedagogical data from their context.

Bereday's third stage, that of juxtaposition, establishes similarities and differences in two educational situations in a 'preliminary matching of the data secured from the first two stages in order to prepare the way for comparison' (Jones, 1971, p. 90). Surprisingly, only at this stage does Bereday suggest the formation of a hypothesis. Such an approach is problematic because the scope of a study must somehow be delimited, and the formation of hypotheses allows an investigation to proceed with a measure of focus and specificity. Therefore, tentative hypotheses about the implementation of language-in-education policies have helped to guide this research during the document collection phase and throughout the case study site visits.

The final stage in Bereday's methodology is that of simultaneous comparison, aiming for an 'objective, consistent conclusion – that is some proof that the hypothesis established is tenable'. Bereday is right in warning at this stage against the danger of 'straining for symmetry where none exists', although this lack of alignment may result in what he claims is an 'inferior' method of illustrative comparison (Jones, 1971, p. 91). In this study, however, one must appreciate the complexities of language policy and practice and recognize that both symmetry and difference, when carefully analysed, can lead to meaningful insights.

While Bereday's framework is a useful guide to approaching the research process, Edmund King's contextually sensitive methodology, as explored in *Education and Social Change* (1966), gives insight into the 'tools' a study requires. His preference for a pragmatic approach – 'he accepts what will work' – sufficiently recognizes the individual character of each educational situation (Jones, 1971, p. 128). Although King's procedures of analysis have been criticized for their supposed lack of methodological rigour, they are exceedingly useful for this study. His insistence on understanding the 'cultural envelope' in a given situation is especially critical in a multi-lingual, multi-ethnic study, as is his (and others') insistence on an awareness of cultural bias. Additionally, King's use of 'patterns' to analyse data seems to allow for a more nuanced analysis than Bereday's search for correspondences and symmetry. These patterns help to illuminate complex relationships between language-in-education policies and practices and facilitate meaningful comparison.

The purposes of this research are multiple. In drawing upon Theisen & Adams' classification of comparative research (1990), this study could be categorized as analytical, descriptive, and exploratory. Because it defies a simple classification, multiple methods of data collection are needed to accurately comprehend and later compare the given educational situations. A qualitative case study approach enables an exploration of the complexities of language policy and practice in education.

2. Research Strategy and Methods

Case studies were chosen as the most appropriate research strategy in determining the practical application of these language-in-education policies. In recognizing that the '"experimental science" type approaches are ill-suited to the complexity, embedded character, and specificity of real-life phenomena' (Gillham, 2000, p. 6), this study uses qualitative methods to reach a thorough understanding of educational situations. This approach, which stresses the importance of contextual variables, is especially suited for comparative study because 'one of [case studies'] strengths is that they observe effects in real contexts, recognizing that context is a powerful determinant of both causes and effects' (Cohen et al, 2000, p. 180). A multiple-method approach including interviews and observation aims to provide evidence for description as well as interpretation. The purpose of these 'instrumental' case studies (Stake, 1994) is to gain insight into the issue of language policy and implementation through the examination of two educational situations.

Case studies, however, present certain challenges to the researcher. The amount of information available from a given site in a qualitative study is vast, and the selections that a researcher makes may lead to distortion through the inclusion or exclusion of certain data (Bassey, 1999). Also, the generalizability of the findings – the extent to which one can draw conclusions that apply to a wider context – is often seen as limited (Walford, 2001). Despite these and other potential weaknesses of this type of research (see Nisbet & Watt, 1984), the case study remains well-suited to explore the relationships between social, political, and linguistic factors, those 'complexities that are beyond the scope of more 'controlled' approaches' (Gillham, 2000, p. 11).

In recognition of the benefits of comparative analysis, two sites were selected for case studies: 'Forest Hill' Primary in England and 'Shady Ridge' Elementary in the United States (in Texas), both located in large urban areas and serving multi-lingual and multi-ethnic populations. (The schools' names have been changed to ensure anonymity.) Within each school, one specific level was selected for intense study. Year two in England and first grade in the United States were selected as comparable, based upon the following rationale:

- Both represent the second year of each school's curriculum

- Both are within the first stage of the compulsory school curriculum, preparing pupils for their first national or state assessments
- Pupils are the same age (six or seven years old).

These case studies do not act as 'representative' of their respective states or countries; instead, they are significant in themselves as examples of diverse, multi-lingual schools. As Walford explains, 'choosing a site that is interesting or important in itself is the only safe way to ensure that results have meaning beyond the particular case selected' (2001, p. 17). Therefore, the case studies are valuable in showing the *significance* of language policy implementations, not the *frequency* of certain implementations in a larger sample (Cohen et al, 2000). Generalization, while not the goal of this study, must be left to the readers. Indeed, Gillham believes that generalizations are '[often] suspect because there are too many elements that are *specific* to [a] group or institution' (2000, p. 6). This study does, however, attempt to achieve 'transferability' through the process of 'thick description' (Walford, 2001). 'Thick description', a term pioneered by American social anthropologist Clifford Geertz, can be achieved through attention to, reflection on, and written analysis of 'the fine grain of what you are observing' (Gillham, 2000, p. 19).

One method used to gather data in this study was teacher and administrator interviews. At each site, interviews were conducted with teachers, assistants, school administrators, and coordinators at the school and LEA/district levels who work primarily with minority language pupils. The purpose of these interviews was to discover the subjects' perceptions of the practice of language policy in their classroom, school, or LEA/district, respectively. The interviews were conducted using a semi-structured 'interview guide approach', in which questions were outlined in advance but flexibility to alter the sequence or the wording of the questions during the interview remained (Patton, 1980). Although possibly reducing the strict comparability of data, this interview structure, using open-ended questions, fostered a more 'natural' environment and allowed respondents to expand upon relevant issues that may have been unanticipated by the researcher. Pilot interviews were conducted to determine the relevance and comprehensiveness of the questions, and subsequent improvements were made. Interviews were tape-recorded with participant permission and later partially transcribed. In the analysis of the data, the transcriptions and the original recordings were used to capture the extra-linguistic factors (such as interruptions) in the interview situation that might have affected interviewees' responses (Walford, 2001).

Certain shortcomings of interview data make it necessary to combine interviewing with another research method: observation. Interviews, especially those that gather teacher and administrator 'perceptions', can be limited by individual biases, memory, and even evasions and self-deception (Walford, 2001). In recognizing the intractability of such factors, Kitwood (1977) suggests that these interviews are therefore representative of 'everyday life', in which individuals are inextricable from their biases (cited in Cohen et al, 2000). Nevertheless, one must recognize that beliefs and perceptions expressed in an interview may differ from classroom practice.

Therefore, to contextualize teachers' and administrators' interviews, observations were made in the classroom of each interviewed teacher at the selected year or grade level. Observation is invaluable in qualitative research; Cohen et al even believe that 'at the heart of every case study lies a method of observation' (2000, p. 185). Observations were completed using a 'semi-structured' approach, in which an agenda of topics was determined before the observation but narrative note-taking reflected a variety of issues that arose in the lessons. In these observations, the researcher undertook the role of an 'observer as participant'. By assisting in the classroom, the researcher helped to reduce the 'reactivity effects' of her presence. However, periodic detachment from class activities allowed for adequate *in situ* note-taking, which was later complemented by expanded notes recorded after each observation. These observations provided for an amount of 'immersion' in the classrooms, which allowed the researcher to differentiate between perceptions and practice and which helped to 'facilitate generation of "thick descriptions" which lead ... to accurate explanation and interpretation of events rather than relying on the researcher's own inferences' (Cohen et al, 2000, p. 311).

Qualitative research methods are often criticized as being subjective and easily influenced by the researcher's conscious or unconscious preconceptions or prejudices. In order to counter this tendency, multiple methods of data collection were employed, and several data sources were used to support any single analysis or hypothesis. Also, the process of gathering information from documents as well as multiple interviewees holding a variety of positions within the school systems helped to ensure that the data found were truly 'representative' of the situation. By integrating data from national, state, LEA/district, school, and classroom levels, this study employed multi-level analysis, which 'facilitates more comprehensive and possibly more accurate presentation of the phenomenon [addressed]' (Bray & Thomas, 1995, p. 484). In the case study descriptions and comparisons, every attempt was made to triangulate data and integrate them into a 'chain of evidence', in which each element or finding was supported by or related to other types of evidence (Yin, 1994; Gillham, 2000).

Several efforts were made to ensure that those individuals and institutions studied were represented fairly and accurately and that participants' rights and concerns were respected. All participants' names have been changed to ensure anonymity. Teachers and administrators voluntarily participated in interviews and observations and have agreed to allow the researcher to keep all identifying information, including documents, observations, transcribed interviews, and the tapes themselves, on the condition that they remain confidential and in the researcher's possession. Additionally, participants have given permission for the researcher to publish any information obtained through interviews and observations.

3. The Case Studies

The following case study analyses are the result of one-week investigations at each site. Interviewees have been coded with a letter and a designated number, which are used in the case studies to identify sources for quotations or specific facts. Participants from Forest Hill (Chapter Five) are identified with the letter 'F', and those from Shady Ridge (Chapter Six) with the letter 'S' (see Appendices E and M for more demographic information about these participants, and Appendices H and P for excerpts from their taped interviews).

Although every effort has been made to triangulate the data presented in this study, the reader must be aware of the sources from which the information in the following chapters was gathered. The data resulting from the interviews must be understood as teachers' and administrators' *perceptions* of a situation, rather than simply its factual representation. Also, because the scale of this study is restricted, this analysis does not attempt to be representative of other schools or of the countries as a whole; the case study has been conducted with the hope that it 'might illuminate the process of schooling elsewhere, but not with the intention that any specific findings should be generalizable' (Vulliamy et al, 1990, pp. 12-13).

CHAPTER 5

England Case Study: Forest Hill Primary

1. Pupil and Community Characteristics

Forest Hill Primary School is located in one of England's major urban centers, which includes a substantial university population. The school is situated a few miles away from the city's central commercial district in an area which recently underwent significant revitalization. According to an OFSTED report (2001a), approximately 41.6% of pupils apply for free school meals at Forest Hill, in comparison to the national average of 18.6%.

The pupil population of Forest Hill is remarkably diverse, ethnically, linguistically, and culturally. Over 97% of the school's 457 pupils do not speak English as a first language; many of these pupils were born in England, however, and the most proficient of them do not receive specific EAL support. The first language of the majority of pupils at Forest Hill is Urdu/Punjabi (over 66%), although pupils speaking Arabic and Malaysian/Indonesian comprise 17% and 7% of the population, respectively. The Urdu/Punjabi-speaking pupils, mostly from families from the Mirpur region of Pakistan, are usually second- or third-generation British (F1). In contrast, the Arabic-speaking pupils are almost exclusively from Libya and are more likely to be recent arrivals to England. The parents of both Arabic- and Malaysian/Indonesian-speaking pupils tend to be enrolled in programmes at the local university for a limited time; these pupils are therefore much more transitory and rarely complete all seven years of primary schooling at Forest Hill (F1, 3). (For more information on the languages spoken by Forest Hill's pupils, see Appendix F.)

Community schools are significant in the lives of many EAL pupils at Forest Hill. Because most of the Arabic-speaking pupils will be returning to Libya before the end of their educational careers, their private after-school Arabic classes assume great importance (F2). Most Urdu/Punjabi speakers attend Koranic school at one of the local mosques in the evening (F1, 4). Some staff at Forest Hill show concern that the time and effort pupils spend in these schools, when combined with their

English schooling, leave too little time for socialization and creative play (F6). Arabic-speaking pupils must learn the Libyan curriculum and pass national examinations so that they can make the transition back into formal schooling at the appropriate level when they return to their home country. As a result, some staff members believe that the parents of these pupils place little importance on the education provided at Forest Hill (F1, 2). For Urdu/Punjabi-speaking pupils, the hours spent engaged in Koranic memorization at 'mosque schools' is seen by one staff member as possibly detrimental to pupils' English reading and comprehension skills (F1).

The city council's Ethnic Minority Achievement Service (EMAS, known as the 'Service') supports many such community schools through small financial contributions. In return for this modest funding, the Service inspects community schools to ensure that health and safety regulations are met (F7). However, the Arabic school that pupils attend operates independently of this funding. Therefore, it is not subject to such oversight, and the Service is unable to monitor the activities in which the school is engaged (F2).

Cultural factors also appear to affect parents' roles in the school community. While teachers and administrators desire more parent involvement in the school, they explain that such involvement is restricted by a variety of factors, including:

- A 'respect' for teachers that prevents parents from 'interfering' in school matters
- A linguistic and/or intellectual insecurity that prevents parents from participating in their children's curricular learning (F4, 5, 6).

Additionally, some staff members note that parents' maintenance of close ties with relatives internationally leads them to withdraw their children from school for extended periods of time for overseas visits. Many staff believe that both the lack of parental support and the absences resulting from family visits negatively affect pupils' performance.

2. Recent Reorganizations and Changes

Forest Hill recently underwent significant structural and physical changes. It was originally two separate institutions – Forest Hill Infants School and Forest Hill Junior School – which merged in April 1997, doubling the size of the primary school and necessitating the hiring of additional staff members. Additionally, the school relocated to a new building in the autumn of 2001. Although the move resulted in improved facilities and resources, the school's budget has subsequently been somewhat restricted (F4).

3. EMAS Staff and Policy

Of the sixty-one full- and part-time teaching and associate staff at Forest Hill, at least eighteen are bilingual, the majority in Urdu/Punjabi (see Appendix F). Six members are identified as EMAS staff: those working specifically with ethnic minority and EAL pupils, and (all but one) employed through Ethnic Minority Achievement Grant funding. The Forest Hill EMAS department includes:

- One full-time coordinator (qualified teacher)
- One part-time support teacher (qualified teacher)
- One full-time Arabic-speaking bilingual instructor
- One part-time Arabic-speaking bilingual instructor (funded directly by the school, not the EMAS grant)
- One full-time Urdu/Punjabi-speaking bilingual instructor
- One part-time Urdu/Punjabi-speaking bilingual nursery nurse (a teaching assistant who supports pupils in the early primary years).

Forest Hill's EMAS coordinator identifies her role as primarily non-instructional; she manages staff and works on school-wide EAL initiatives, such as curriculum modification. She believes the role of all EMAS staff is to 'team teach, to provide support materials, to work with targeted pupils, and above all [to] raise achievement' (F1). The bilingual instructors and nursery nurse identify their responsibilities as:

- Assisting groups of pupils in class
- Simultaneously translating lessons in class
- Listening to individual pupils' oral reading
- Providing oral translations as part of national assessment modifications
- Translating written documents
- Liaising with parents
- Providing pastoral support for pupils and families (F2, 5, 9, 10).

This final area of responsibility was identified by one instructor as the 'majority' of her job (F2). According to the most recent timetables of the EMAS staff members (excluding that of the coordinator), over 85% of their schedules are devoted to supporting pupils in mainstream classes.

Surprisingly, at both the Service and the school level, there is little conception of a coherent 'EAL policy' (F1, 7). Because the national government does not provide specific directives regarding the educational arrangements for EAL pupils, the Service has created a flexible policy of its own. According to the deputy head of the Service, EMAS in schools should be:

> very much a support service; we support the teachers. Our policy is we don't work in isolation. We don't take children out of the classroom. That's a sweeping statement, because it

does happen ... but as our stated policy, we prefer in-class support, working in groups, working in partnership with the teacher. (F7)

The Service's official handbook encourages bilingual instructors to use pupils' first languages to 'enable them to access the curriculum', but they are not obliged to support the *development* of first-language skills.

The Service provides guidance and support to Forest Hill's EMAS staff through an induction program for new staff and mandatory in-service training. Curricular concerns, however, are the responsibility of the specific school (F8). The Service monitors schools' use of the EMAS grant and their EMAS personnel through annual data collection, which categorizes pupils by ethnicity, English ability, and pastoral need.

4. Implementation of Language-in-Education Policies for Non-Native English Speakers

To clearly envisage how pupils are affected by these notions of 'language policy', the following data are presented at both a school level and within a single grade level. These findings, collected through interviews and classroom observations, relate to the areas of English-language development, first-language development, and assessment.

The grade level selected for focused observation is year two, which is taught at Forest Hill by two teachers, known subsequently as teacher F3 and teacher F6. Teacher F3 has thirty pupils in her class, including twenty-six EAL pupils, the majority of whom are Urdu/Punjabi speakers. The composition of teacher F6's class is ethnically similar, and only one of her thirty pupils speaks English as a first language. (For further demographic information, see Appendix G.) Teacher F3 has a monolingual English-speaking EMAS support teacher one day per week and a (non-EMAS) bilingual 'learning mentor' three days per week. Teacher F6 has a full-time classroom assistant who speaks Urdu/Punjabi, but her pupils do not receive any in-class support from EMAS staff. The week after the case study was conducted, an EMAS support teacher was scheduled to begin working with her class, but teacher F6 was unsure what the purpose of this new intervention would be.

(a) English Language Development and Literacy

The primary vehicle for formal English language development at Forest Hill is the National Literacy Strategy (NLS), which was implemented in every classroom observed in a manner consistent with the recommendations in the National Literacy Framework. Yet many teachers and administrators express dissatisfaction with the NLS, mostly as a result of falling Key Stage Two national assessment results the previous year, particularly in reading comprehension (F1, 4, 6). As a result, improving pupils' reading comprehension has become a school-wide initiative. The most visible aspect of this initiative is the school's literacy working group, which is attempting to significantly modify the Literacy Hour with measures specifically addressing EAL pupils' language development needs.

It is significant to note that the working group received substantial guidance from a teacher-initiated, university-guided research project. One of the teacher-researchers recalled her dissatisfaction with the NLS: 'We were just concerned that we taught the same strategy to every single child', despite variations in pupils' proficiency in English (F8). As a result, the teachers conducted a small-scale study of pupils' writing, in which they quantified and categorized errors by their grammatical features and by the first languages of the pupils making those errors. From their analysis, the researchers identified several mistakes common to pupils from all language backgrounds. The literacy working group is now integrating certain 'grammar rules' into their programme to address these errors.

Several teachers believe that the NLS generally lacks the grammatical focus that EAL pupils need to develop their English literacy skills. Some, however, believe they do not have the linguistic knowledge to identify the specific grammatical shortcomings of the strategy: 'without having been taught English grammar ourselves as teachers, we wouldn't necessarily pick up on [them]' (F3).

The modifications to the NLS proposed by the working group are currently being developed into a detailed curriculum that includes a greater diversity of texts as well as an increased focus on grammar, speaking, and listening. These developments have not yet been implemented, although the working group hopes to begin pilot tests in the near future (F1, 3, 4).

In year two, teachers try to address pupils' specific language development needs in the Literacy Hour largely through the use of ability groups and targeted instruction, rather than curriculum modification. Teacher F3 explains that the ability to provide small-group or individual instruction is restricted because of staff availability:

> It's a human resources issue as well as a strategy issue. If you
> have enough people, you can sort your groups out and
> somebody else can take the group and teach from the strategy
> in a different way, but when it's just you in your class, you
> have to [teach to] the sixty percent majority. (F3)

Despite the use of bilingual support staff in these lessons, all aspects of the Literacy Hour lessons observed in both year-two classrooms were conducted completely in English.

In teacher F3's classroom, the EMAS support teacher was observed assisting pupils in whole-group sessions by sitting on the floor near a group of EAL pupils whom she later identified as recent arrivals to England. She constructed graphic representations of the main points of the teacher's lecture, which she then showed to those pupils. Additionally, she questioned some of these pupils individually as the teacher spoke. In small groups, she worked with the higher-ability pupils to complete a reading comprehension task designed by the classroom teacher. According to teacher F3, her bilingual learning mentor also works with a variety of pupils in whole-group sessions. In contrast, during small-group work, she assists the pupils identified as having lower ability levels.

Teacher F6's assistant was observed working with a variety of children in the Literacy Hour, targeting those the teacher has identified as 'low ability'. During whole-group sessions, the assistant monitored pupils' behavior and encouraged pupils to contribute to the discussion. The teacher assigned the assistant to work with one of the lower ability sets of pupils during small-group work.

Year-two teachers employ a variety of strategies to help pupils acquire English literacy skills, by providing visual and auditory stimuli during the Literacy Hour lessons. However, teachers use these techniques in an effort to cater to all learning styles rather than to address EAL pupils' specific linguistic needs. These teacher behaviors relate directly to their lack of initial and continuing training in EAL, as well as the lack of time provided to plan jointly with EMAS or other bilingual support staff. Both of these issues are discussed in detail in sections 5.5c and 5.5e below.

(b) First-Language Development and Literacy

First languages are employed primarily by EMAS instructors and other bilingual staff to facilitate curricular access rather than to develop first-language literacy skills, in contrast to the bilingual program described in Chapter Six. EMAS staff were observed using first languages orally (and with Arabic, in written form) to enhance pupils' comprehension and to encourage EAL pupils' participation in English-medium lessons. EMAS staff worked in whole-class, small-group, and withdrawal situations and sometimes used both languages to teach a concept or provide an explanation. The amount of code-switching between languages appeared to vary according to specific pupils' language abilities.

The EMAS coordinator and staff show enthusiasm for incorporating first languages in mainstream classroom teaching, but this does not systematically occur school-wide. Many bilingual staff, EMAS and otherwise, are willing to simultaneously translate lessons into pupils' first languages, but a general lack of teacher interest for Urdu/Punjabi whole-class translation has limited this strategy (F1, 9). The full-time

Arabic-speaking assistant, in contrast, is widely valued for her first-language skills and her in-class support of smaller groups of pupils.

School-wide initiatives to incorporate pupils' first languages are largely restricted to non-curricular activities. Most teachers mention that a variety of celebrations and various extracurricular activities occur throughout the year that address pupils' cultural and religious backgrounds. Urdu/Punjabi- and Arabic-speaking EMAS staff frequently produce multi-lingual signs and translations of letters to parents. In an effort to provide more structured first-language development, an Urdu language class was proposed as a lunchtime extracurricular club, but the initiative has not yet been approved by the governing body (F1, 4).

In year two, both teachers have bilingual support available in their classrooms, but their use of these resources varies. Teacher F3 utilizes the Urdu/Punjabi skills of her non-EMAS bilingual learning mentor to simultaneously translate mathematics lessons on a regular basis. She explains that they tried the same strategy in the Literacy Hour but felt it was not effective. In general, however, teacher F3 identifies bilingual support as the most effective intervention which EMAS can provide for her pupils.

Teacher F6 did not incorporate first-language use into the structure of any lessons observed. She believes that her pupils generally do not require first-language support: 'I've not got any children that really struggle ... they're all pretty fluent' (F6). In all lessons observed, her full-time bilingual assistant used only English to speak with pupils. However, teacher F6 did explain that her assistant was going to begin simultaneously translating science and mathematics lessons in the future.

(c) Assessment of EAL Pupils

Pupils at Forest Hill are assessed through a combination of instruments, but the National Curriculum assessments (SATs), taken in year two and year six, receive most of the teachers' and administrators' attention, just as state assessments do at Shady Ridge. At the discretion of the EMAS coordinator and the senior management team, EAL pupils can participate in SATs examinations in English or in their first language, with the exception of the reading and writing tests, which must be completed in English. However, unlike Texas' state assessments, SATs are not provided in a translated format; the bilingual instructors must orally translate the questions during the assessments. Depending on the pupils' competence in their first language and English, these bilingual instructors may also translate the pupils' responses back into English. Such a process is time-consuming, and translations of 'optional' SATs assessments in years three, four, and five do not occur because they would further restrict time available for EMAS to support children in classrooms (F4).

The preparation for SATs assessments also affects the deployment of EMAS personnel. The head teacher reports that these staff spend a large proportion of their time in year two and year six classrooms helping pupils to prepare for these examinations, although she acknowledges that such a strategy is 'really ... not the best use of a bilingual worker' (F4).

SATs are seen by some teachers and administrators as problematic for EAL pupils in both their content and cultural focus. For example, some teachers believe that these assessments specifically disadvantage EAL pupils because they are unable to measure intelligence as distinct from language ability (F1). Also, there is frustration that although SATs are designed for a 'middle-class', non-EAL population who have had lifelong exposure to English, Forest Hill's assessment scores are still measured against those of such a 'normative' population (F4).

EAL pupils are assessed annually to determine their placement on an English-language development (STEP) scale, created by the Northern Association of Support Services for Equality and Achievement (NASSEA; see Chapter Three). Testing pupils according to this scale is a time-consuming task, requiring EMAS staff to spend at least two weeks out of classes each time the assessment is given (F1). Additionally, the value of the scale is seen as limited; 'it needs to be incorporated into the other assessments going on to give a full picture [of an EAL pupil's abilities]' (F1).

The only other EAL-specific assessments at Forest Hill that focus on language development are pupil records that EMAS staff are supposed to maintain each half-term for the EAL pupils with whom they work. Some of the EMAS staff admit that these records are not always kept current because of the time necessary to complete them. Additionally, they believe the assessment is of limited value because the records do not allow space for sufficiently specific comments (F1, 10).

In year two classrooms, pupils are assessed every half-term in English and mathematics, and after each unit in science (F3, 6). The assessment measures and benchmarks, however, are neither designed nor adapted for an EAL population. There is no evidence that classroom teachers are involved in the STEP language assessments or the EMAS half-term records.

Both teachers in year two view the SATs assessments as problematic for EAL pupils. Teachers F3 and F6 both believe that their pupils' vocabulary and comprehension skills are not at the standard required for the SATs. Also, teacher F6 thinks that the restrictions related to formal assessment disadvantage her pupils; while rephrasing questions would, she believes, allow pupils to understand and respond correctly, testing regulations do not allow such a practice.

5. Factors Affecting Language-in-Education Policy Implementation

(a) School Funding and Institutional Support

The EMAS Service, schools, and individual teachers are all affected by recent and anticipated changes in government funding for EAL and ethnic minority pupils. A representative of the Service identifies the mercurial nature of government support as the organization's greatest difficulty:

> The challenge we always have is we rely entirely on central government money, which is at the behest of politicians. If we have a change of government, we'll be under threat again. We spend most of our existence under the threat of, if not extinction, then certainly considerable cuts. (F7)

Although current governmental policy has continued to support ethnic minority pupils, a growing concern is that EMAS funding will soon be streamlined into general school budgets (F4, 7). As a result, funding for ethnic minority and EAL pupils would no longer be 'ring-fenced' and schools would have much greater flexibility in how they provide support for EAL pupils, with less oversight from the DfES or the Service (F4). As Forest Hill's head teacher explains, 'I know that on the ground level ... heads and governing bodies will have to make some hard decisions ... which concerns me that our EAL pupils could miss out' (F4).

Also, the manner in which EMAS funding is devolved to schools has resulted in a fractured structure of monitoring and implementation. The government transfers EMAS funding directly to the Service, which then allocates this money to the schools according to the guidelines mentioned in Chapter Three. While most schools in this city choose to 'buy back' their EMAS staff through the Service, five schools do not, instead spending the funding according to their own priorities. Although the Service is charged with monitoring the implementation of the EMAS funds, its ability to intervene is limited:

> If a school is doing something that we don't approve of, we can tell them, we can make noises, but at the end of the day the money is with them. They can tell us to take our staff out, and they'll just sort their own thing out. (F7)

In such a case, the effectiveness of the Service is constrained by the school's ability to opt out of staffing and funding arrangements.

Because EMAS funding amounts are determined on an annual basis, demographic changes caused by a transitory school population or declining enrollment can drastically alter staff allocation from year to year. The temporary nature of this funding has resulted in shortages of qualified EMAS staff because teachers are often discouraged from leaving the relative stability of mainstream classroom teaching (F4). As one EMAS teacher explained, 'I've always thought it's a job you don't go into if you want a career, to be honest' (F1).

(b) School Resources

EMAS funding at Forest Hill supports staff salaries, but other resources for EAL pupils must be provided by the school itself. At a time when the budget has 'reduced flexibility' because of a recent building project (F4), the lack of money, time, and space allotted to the EMAS department restricts their activities.

The limited EMAS budget, combined with the high costs of bilingual resources such as dictionaries, books, visual aids, and software, prevents the school from purchasing what some staff consider 'adequate' bilingual resources (F1, 2, 3). The library and some classrooms have a selection of dual-language books and resources, but some interviewees believe this supply is limited in relation to the proportion of pupils at Forest Hill who speak English as an additional language.

EMAS staff demonstrate willingness to produce their own materials and resources for pupils and teachers, but the time and space to do so are limited. There is no physical area allotted solely to the EMAS staff; they must share their workroom and do not have access to it for a portion of the week. Additionally, the time available for creating resources is limited: 'We could make so much ourselves ... but we're only allowed half an hour [for our weekly EMAS meeting]. If we want more time, the head suggests we stay after school' (F1).

Despite these difficulties, EMAS teachers and bilingual instructors have reported creating a variety of dual-language resources. Bilingual instructors were observed translating and creating signs in Arabic and Urdu for use in classrooms. Additionally, the full-time Arabic-speaking bilingual instructor reports that she is using portions of the Arabic community school's curriculum to re-teach and reinforce concepts taught in Forest Hill's English-medium classes. Such efforts, undertaken at the bilingual instructor's initiative, are not supported by a school-wide strategy for first-language or EAL resource development.

(c) Professional Development and Teacher Training

All teachers, instructors, and nursery nurses employed through the EMAS grant at Forest Hill are given initial induction training as well as four-and-a-half days of ongoing training per year. Topics addressed have included staff management, social inclusion, achievement, ICT, language development, home-school links, and racial equality. Although these sessions, provided by the Service, are also open to mainstream teachers and assistants, no mainstream staff interviewed had attended any of them. However, twelve Forest Hill teachers have registered for an Urdu course to be offered in the future (F7). As in the US case study, EMAS staff responses to this training are variable; one bilingual instructor notes that her on-the-job experience has been more valuable than her training, but another finds that the quality of the sessions has been improving (F1, 5).

The lack of an EAL component in initial teacher training in England has led to a situation at Forest Hill in which mainstream teachers are largely uninformed about EAL pupils' specific language needs. Neither of the year two teachers report having any specific EAL training or experience before beginning her teaching career. Teacher F6 remembers: 'We didn't get anything, really. I didn't really know what EAL was before coming [to Forest Hill].' Such a situation, according to one EMAS staff member, results in a need for school-wide training on these issues (F1).

Mainstream classroom teachers at Forest Hill are trained through a 'cascade approach', in which selected teachers receive external training in a given area with the understanding that they will share this expertise with other staff upon their return. As a result, teachers must seek out this expertise or petition for specific training:

> So unless you actually go and seek out somebody and say, 'I really need some help' or, 'I really need to go on a course', then you tend not to receive any training, not as a matter of course. (F3)

In any case, some teachers explain that this external training rarely addresses the needs of teachers who have EAL pupils: 'There aren't any experts to train teachers like us ... you're desperate for the advice, but there often isn't anyone to give it to you' (F3). External training, then, is generally not perceived as helpful in developing mainstream teachers' expertise in EAL issues or strategies.

In addition to external training for both mainstream and EMAS staff, teachers also attend school-wide training sessions. At Forest Hill during the first half of the 2002-2003 academic year, two internal sessions for mainstream teachers were provided by the EMAS staff on their roles and responsibilities. Additionally, the results of the teacher-led research in EAL writing (see section 4a on English Language Development and Literacy, above) were presented. However, mainstream teachers and members of EMAS staff desire more specific training about EAL issues in the following areas:

- English grammar and linguistics
- The structure and vocabulary of pupils' first languages
- Pupils' cultural and religious backgrounds
- The role of community schools (F1, 3, 6, 10).

With the exception of the forthcoming Urdu course, neither the Service nor the school has yet provided training which specifically addresses these areas, and so individual teachers must currently seek these types of expertise informally or from other sources outside the school.

(d) School Leadership

The senior management team at Forest Hill includes the head teacher, two assistants, and two curriculum coordinators. While the governing body and the senior management team support school development through participation in initiatives and training, few of these appear to specifically target EAL pupils or their language development needs. The head teacher expresses great satisfaction that Forest Hill has become involved in a variety of community and government initiatives traditionally undertaken only by schools with higher socio-economic status or more homogeneous populations (F4). Teachers also believe that these programmes are beneficial to Forest Hill pupils. However, teachers and EMAS staff do not mention senior management as a specific source of support for EAL teaching strategies. Although many EMAS staff note the importance of management decisions in determining whole-school policies, such guidance in EAL-related issues is not evident (F1, 5, 10).

(e) Professional Relations and the Status of EMAS Staff

In contrast to ESL and bilingual teachers at Shady Ridge, many EMAS staff at Forest Hill feel the need to 'prove themselves' and their worth in the classroom. In describing this relationship among staff, an official with the Service explains that, 'I think the only thing that teachers value is a teacher in front of the class ... [it's] up to the individual [EMAS staff member] really to show proof of credibility' (F7). Because EMAS staff do not have responsibility for an entire classroom as mainstream teachers do, they may be perceived as less valuable. Since they are neither autonomous classroom teachers nor simply assistants, their role seems to be uncertain:

> You're going in just like in some schools a parent ... or a
> teaching assistant or a learning mentor [might] ... and so
> [pupils are] used to adults going in, but their perception is,
> '*That's* the teacher. All the other adults are not teachers' [my
> emphasis]. (F1)

This ambiguity seems to be, in some part, a result of ignorance about EMAS staff and their qualifications; for example, one Forest Hill classroom teacher was unaware that an EMAS support teacher in her class is, in fact, a qualified teacher as well.

Further ambiguity regarding EMAS teachers, instructors, and nursery nurses results from the terms of their employment. Although employed by the Service, EMAS staff are directly accountable to head teachers. Such a conflict in loyalties can result in a situation in which:

> EMAS employees know that if they don't please their head teachers they may be out of the school. And if a head teacher wants them to, say, do cover, because a teacher's away, [which] they should not be doing because it devalues their role ... they'll play along with it ... They might be asked to work with children who have got learning difficulties and special educational needs rather than children who are ethnic minorities. (F7)

In fact, several EMAS staff at Forest Hill express the concern that they are sometimes mis-assigned by teachers to work with pupils who do not have EAL needs.

Opportunities for EMAS staff and classroom teachers to plan lessons together is viewed as an important aspect of integrating EMAS support into classrooms, but a lack of time often restricts efforts to undertake joint planning. Teacher F3 is dissatisfied with the insufficient time available to plan lesson objectives and activities with support staff. Currently, she may not have any opportunity to jointly plan or even discuss the day's lesson before class begins:

> That's not satisfactory to me. I need to know that [if] someone's coming in that I know what they're doing [and] they know what I want them to do ... Having the time to organize that and plan that together ... is really lacking at the moment ... I don't know where we'd fit it in. (F3)

While the head teacher supports this idea of partnership, she is unable to *insist* that teachers and EMAS staff plan together, because there is no time in the school day officially allotted to do so (F4). Additionally, full-time bilingual instructors work with multiple teachers and year levels in a single week; planning with each teacher seems a practical impossibility. All EMAS teachers and instructors express frustration that planning time with classroom teachers is very limited.

The viability of planning and teaching in partnership also depends on the personalities of the teachers and instructors involved. Just as teachers vary in their desire to incorporate EMAS support into their lessons, not all EMAS staff favour the idea of assuming a stronger classroom presence (F1, 3, 5, 10).

(f) Staffing Allocations

Although Forest Hill has hired an additional bilingual instructor, all staff interviewed believe that there are still too few EMAS staff to assist all EAL pupils adequately. As a result, pupils who are underachieving and/or who are preparing for SATs assessments are more likely to receive EMAS support than those with the lowest English-language abilities (F1, 4).

For new pupils with little or no spoken English, an EMAS staff member provides a short induction period in which pupils are acclimatized to the school environment and taught survival English skills. The length and regularity of this support, however, is restricted by the substantial number of new arrivals (F1). Any type of subsequent individual tutoring or assessment of EAL pupils is similarly restricted by the scarcity of EMAS staff for in-class support.

(g) Complexities of First-Language Use

Just as Leung et al (1997) seek to dismantle the myth of a homogeneous, idealized 'native' speaker, it is equally clear that the first-language abilities of EAL pupils at Forest Hill vary widely and therefore require diverse educational responses. Pupils' first-language abilities are affected by the length of time they have lived in England, their academic background in their first language, and the dialect of the language they speak.

Although Pakistani pupils at Forest Hill who have just arrived in England are often literate in Urdu/Punjabi, the first-language skills of many second- and third-generation immigrants are considered weak. There is a fear that these pupils are becoming 'deficient' in both their first language and English (F7), but no successful attempts have been made within the LEA or Forest Hill to address first-language literacy within the *formal* school environment. Moreover, it is unclear from the information collected during the investigation to what extent pupils and their parents value bi-literacy. An interviewee notes that in Urdu/Punjabi-speaking communities, some families may value English literacy more highly than literacy in their first language (F7).

Just as the first-language abilities of pupils may vary, not all speakers of a language may share the same dialect. The Arabic-speaking bilingual instructors use regional dialects of the language that are different from those of the EAL pupils at Forest Hill. One instructor explains that, although she has an oral and written knowledge of 'Standard Arabic' in addition to her regional dialect, pupils typically do not learn the standard form of Arabic until the later grades of primary school (F2). As a result, the instructors have to make significant changes in their lexicon to facilitate mutual comprehension.

6. Conclusion

Forest Hill's significant ethnic minority and EAL populations require that the school adapts, as a whole, to these pupils' needs. Some staff members are improving curricular and instructional approaches to address EAL pupils' English-language development. Implementing such initiatives is complicated by a lack of human resources, time, training, and a whole-school awareness of the status and purposes of EMAS support. Although the teachers, instructors, and assistants at both Forest Hill and Shady Ridge exert significant effort to incorporate first languages to a greater extent than policy strictly requires, the support at Forest Hill aims to encourage access to the curriculum rather than to develop first-language literacy for its own sake. In contrast, Shady Ridge implements a bilingual program which aims to promote first-language literacy. Nevertheless, as will be shown in the following chapter, Shady Ridge's teachers share concerns similar to those held by staff at Forest Hill, including a desire for additional training and time to create multi-lingual resources.

CHAPTER 6

United States Case Study: Shady Ridge Elementary

1. Pupil and Community Characteristics

Shady Ridge, an elementary school with over 600 pupils from kindergarten up to grade five, is located in a lower-income section of a middle-income suburban school district in the state of Texas. The large metropolitan area in which the school is located has a population of over one million. A measure of the catchment area's socio-economic level is revealed in the classification of 85.8% of Shady Ridge's pupils as 'economically disadvantaged', compared to a state average of 50.5% (Academic Excellence Indicator System [AEIS], 2002). The population of Shady Ridge, both as a whole and within the LEP programmes, is viewed as moderately stable, without significant influxes of pupils in later grades (S6, 8).

The ethnic diversity of Shady Ridge largely reflects that of the city in which it is located. As a result of historical settlement patterns, the majority of the city's and the school's population is Hispanic (US Census Bureau, 2000). Approximately two-thirds of the pupils at Shady Ridge are identified as Hispanic, although many may have been born in the United States and may not speak Spanish as their first language. Asians and Pacific Islanders, as well as Native Americans, account for a small portion of the school – less than 5% – and some speak English as a native language. Although not a linguistic minority, African-American pupils account for almost 20% of the school's population. The remaining 9.1% of the population consists of white, native speakers of English. (For more demographic information, see Appendices N and O.)

Pupils classified as limited English proficient (LEP) represent almost 40% of Shady Ridge's intake. Over 90% of these pupils speak Spanish as a first language, almost all of whom are enrolled in the school's bilingual programme. Most of these pupils were born in Mexico, but some are from other Latin American countries or the United States. LEP pupils speaking other languages – including Chinese, Hindi, Korean, Thai, Turkish, and Vietnamese – are taught in English as a second language (ESL) classrooms. Some of these pupils receive tutoring in their first language in community schools (S7).

Within the district, five of the thirty-nine elementary schools offer an ESL/bilingual programme. LEP pupils living in other catchment areas are bussed to the closest of these 'cluster' schools if they choose to participate in the ESL/bilingual programme. The LEP population is served by two distinct services in each cluster school, both of which are coordinated by the school's ESL specialist. The bilingual programme provides full-time first-language instruction for Spanish-speaking pupils, while the ESL programme serves all other language groups through English-medium instruction. In this chapter, subsequent references to 'bilingual pupils' refer only to LEP pupils enrolled in the Spanish bilingual programme; other LEP pupils enrolled in the ESL programme are considered 'ESL pupils'.

At each grade level, there is at least one bilingual classroom in which pupils develop literacy and learn curriculum content in Spanish. Pupils identified as LEP who are not Spanish-speakers are grouped together in a designated ESL classroom at each grade level, but because there are sometimes only a few ESL pupils in a given grade level, these classes often include non-LEP pupils as well (S6). Teachers in bilingual and ESL classrooms are certified in one or both fields.

Interestingly, many teachers note significant differences between the ethos of the bilingual and ESL classrooms. Bilingual pupils are generally seen as more obedient and hardworking, as a result of strong familial respect for teachers and education (S9, 10). In contrast, some ESL teachers believe that pupils in their classrooms have more discipline problems than those in bilingual classes (S4, 7, 12).

Several initiatives have been launched at the school level to encourage parental participation, but many teachers at Shady Ridge, like those at Forest Hill, expressed a desire for parents to become more involved. Most teachers believe parents are supportive of their efforts, but parents' active participation in school activities and completing homework is more varied, depending on the individual child (S2, 3, 4). The ESL specialist at Shady Ridge indicates that most parents of LEP pupils are satisfied with the ESL and bilingual classes and do not try to 'exit' their child from the programme so they can participate in a mainstream classroom.

2. Recent Reorganizations and Changes

In the two years before the case study, the staffing structure at Shady Ridge had changed significantly. As part of a school improvement measure in 2000, the staff of Shady Ridge was 'reconstituted'; each teacher was required to reapply for his or her position. The principal, who has been at Shady Ridge since 1999, made significant personnel changes at that time (S11). Some staff believe this measure, combined with strong administrative leadership, has created a more positive school environment (S2, 6, 16).

3. ESL/Bilingual Staff and Policy

Shady Ridge has approximately seventy-one full-time staff, including teachers, administrators, assistants, and professional personnel. According to the principal, more than half have some measure of Spanish-language ability (S11). Over twenty-five of these individuals, all of whom are bilingual in Spanish and English, are directly involved in teaching in the ESL/bilingual programme or supporting its teachers and pupils (S6). These staff include:

- Twelve full-time certified bilingual classroom teachers
- Six full-time certified ESL classroom teachers
- One full-time certified ESL specialist
- Five full-time assistants (uncertified personnel)
- One part-time assistant (uncertified personnel)
- One full-time clerk (uncertified personnel).

In contrast to the staffing arrangement at Forest Hill, each certified ESL/bilingual teacher, with the exception of the ESL specialist, teaches his or her own class on a full-time basis. The assistants support multiple teachers throughout the week, according to a predetermined schedule. These staff members have been affected by a new federal policy which requires that all uncertified personnel earn the equivalent of half of a university degree by December 2005. As a result, many are enrolled in classes and working concurrently. The ESL specialist believes this requirement overburdens these individuals and negatively affects their work (S6).

At the district level, there is a degree of uncertainty as to how to interpret state and national requirements for LEP pupils, although policy at these levels is more precise than national policy recommendations in England. According to one district staff member, the state's education code is somewhat vague in its wording and is often amended, necessitating frequent reinterpretations at the district level (S14). Additionally, the implications of the *No Child Left Behind* legislation (United States Department of Education, 2001) remain unclear to many at the district and school level. There is uncertainty as to:

- The extent to which the new law requires increased accountability for pupils' progress
- The level to which it restricts bilingual programmes
- The manner in which English-language proficiency will be tested (S6, 14).

Some believe, however, that the law seems to be leading toward stricter accountability and a stronger promotion of an all-English agenda (S6, 8). As Shady Ridge's ESL specialist explains:

> In my mind, it's a way of controlling, and who knows in a year or two if [Shady Ridge] will be the way it is ... We're doing the best we can ... but who knows all the different ramifications of how it's going to affect us. (S6)

While much uncertainty remains, the district interprets these state and federal guidelines and assists the cluster schools in implementing them. Although the district's ESL policy model has remained unchanged in recent years, the bilingual education model has undergone several modifications as a result of changing state regulations. At the district level, the ESL/bilingual director, in conjunction with the cluster schools' five ESL specialists, is attempting to develop a 'model' of which curriculum and courses should be offered for LEP pupils at each grade level. The final draft of this framework is still in development (S8). Currently, schools differ in their programme structure and in the age at which they transition pupils out of the bilingual programme into all-English classes. The ESL/bilingual director explains that while there is a need for a coherent district model, the plan must allow each campus to have a degree of flexibility in how it is implemented (S8). In addition to establishing this more comprehensive policy, the director would also like to expand the LEP programme throughout the district and have an ESL/bilingual programme at every elementary school to avoid the bussing of pupils to cluster campuses (S8).

Shady Ridge's specific policy for Spanish-speaking pupils is a late-exit model, in which pupils remain in a bilingual classroom full-time until transitioning into an ESL classroom at fifth grade. For later arrivals, a bilingual class is offered for fifth grade as well. All of the staff members interviewed on this topic believe that this model is more successful than the early-exit model used at the school previously, in which pupils made the transition into ESL classes at third grade. Many staff think pupils are better prepared to enter all-English classrooms after having a longer period in which to consolidate their first-language literacy skills (S1, 2, 3, 6, 11).

4. Implementation of Language-in-Education Policies for Non-Native English Speakers

At Shady Ridge there are ten first-grade classrooms, including three bilingual classes and one ESL class. Bilingual teachers S1, S2, and S3, all native Spanish speakers, each teach fifteen pupils. These teachers share a full-time classroom assistant, who was observed conducting small-group and whole-group activities in the classrooms, helping teachers with procedural tasks, and monitoring individual pupils' behavior. ESL teacher S4 has nine pupils in her class, six of whom are designated as LEP, including Hindi, Spanish, Thai, Turkish, and Vietnamese speakers. She does not have a designated classroom assistant as the bilingual teachers do.

(a) English Language Development and Literacy

Shady Ridge, along with all other elementary schools in the district, uses the externally-developed Four Blocks model as the foundation of its literacy programme (for more information on the structure of Four Blocks, see Appendix K). The district piloted this programme in selected first-grade classrooms in 1997. Gradually, they have expanded its implementation to all elementary grades in every school in the district, and this year is the first in which all grades are utilizing the model (S15). All ESL and bilingual teachers interviewed have had external training in how to use the programme in their classrooms. While bilingual teachers at Shady Ridge have modified or created their own version of the programme in Spanish, no specific or systematic ESL adaptations of the Four Blocks model were observed or mentioned by teachers. Although some ESL teachers find Four Blocks to be adequate for their pupils (S4, 12), one ESL teacher notes that the programme lacks the specific grammar focus that she believes her pupils need (S5).

ESL teachers utilize the mainstream English-medium texts and curriculum, but modify these materials for their pupils as needed. For new pupils who arrive after kindergarten with few or no English skills, the ESL specialist and/or a classroom assistant withdraws them from class for twenty to sixty minutes a day to develop basic communication skills.

In the bilingual programme, the school's curricular model designates thirty minutes for English instruction each day, but even the ESL specialist recognizes that this policy is not implemented uniformly in each classroom (S6). Teachers often tend to minimize English instruction when preparing pupils for Spanish-medium state assessments. As the specialist explains, 'when you have that horrible test looming over you, it's amazing how that runs your curriculum' (S6). For example, the fifth-grade ESL and bilingual teachers sometimes team-teach in a combination of English and Spanish, but they switch entirely to English after state assessments are taken (S5, 17). They do so to prepare pupils to make the transition into all-English classes the following year, when they begin middle school.

In first grade, teacher S4 believes that Four Blocks is appropriate for her ESL pupils because it is a 'literacy frame' which can be adapted to a variety of language abilities with relative ease. She explains that the strategies she uses with her ESL pupils – visuals, repetition, simplification, utilization of prior knowledge, and modeling – are those that she also uses with her non-ESL pupils. Her priorities for developing pupils' English-language skills are to improve her pupils' vocabulary, reading comprehension, and writing abilities (S4).

First-grade bilingual teachers focus on English in an entirely different manner. At this level, no English literacy is taught. Although some pupils occasionally speak to each other or their teacher informally in English, all literacy lessons observed took place in Spanish. However, first-grade pupils were observed attending a library session which occurs once a week, in which they listen to stories and interact with the librarian in English.

The bilingual teachers all use English as a means of informal oral communication throughout the school day, but they differ in the extent to which they report incorporating English as a formal element of their curriculum. Teacher S1 explains that he introduces English little by little in various lessons, especially during the second half of the year. He was observed using English during warm-up activities and during informal conversations with pupils. According to teacher S2, she uses English in her classroom to explain science and social studies concepts, to give instructions, and to communicate with her pupils outside the classroom. She tries to encourage her pupils to develop English 'naturally', and allows them to use it orally when she is teaching in Spanish (S2). She was observed using English orally both to give pupils directions and to respond to pupils' questions when asked in English. Teacher S3 explains that she uses English to reinforce concepts first taught in Spanish, mostly in science and social studies. In lessons observed she used English outside formal instructional time both to clarify instructions and ask questions.

(b) First-Language Development and Literacy

Although the LEP pupils at Shady Ridge speak several languages, only Spanish is formally supported in the school setting. Teachers and staff believe that pupils should be taught in their first languages for a variety of reasons. They identify the following as benefits of first-language literacy:

- First-language skills strengthen second-language development
- Pupils feel more comfortable interacting in their first language, and this helps them make a better transition into the school setting
- The enrichment and improvement of first-language competence is valuable in its own right (S1, 2, 3, 6, 7, 9, 10, 11, 16).

The bilingual programme curriculum follows the state content standards for each academic subject, and pupils complete all reading and writing activities in Spanish. These bilingual pupils usually take all of their state assessments in Spanish until the fifth grade, when some complete examinations in English.

No first-language instruction or interaction takes place in ESL teacher S4's classroom. She explains that the pupils speak to each other only in English, even if they share the same first language. In lessons observed, pupils did not use their first languages in either formal or informal situations. Although teacher S4 does not utilize any aspects of pupils' first languages in the classroom, she believes she is successful in incorporating pupils' cultures through the celebration of festivals and traditions from their home countries.

The first-grade bilingual teachers use a translated and modified version of the Four Blocks model to develop Spanish-language literacy. Teachers S1 and S2 believe that the expectation for bilingual teachers to simply 'translate' the English version of Four Blocks is inappropriate because of the grammatical and structural differences between English and Spanish (S2). As a result, these two teachers worked in partnership to develop their own version of the first-grade literacy curriculum, which has since been shared with other teachers district-wide. In their curriculum, they include texts originally written in Spanish as well as activities that focus on characteristics of Spanish, rather than English, grammar. Teacher S2 is currently creating a Spanish version of the kindergarten curriculum, but it has yet to be implemented (S2). This type of literacy curriculum development has occurred as a result of teachers' own initiatives rather than school- or district-wide efforts, and has not yet been replicated for other grade levels.

Bilingual teacher S1 explains that he uses Spanish for reading, writing, and problem-solving tasks. He believes this is successful because pupils' oral fluency in Spanish is greater and because the language is reinforced at home. He also uses Spanish to foster in pupils a 'complete' knowledge of their first language, avoiding the situation where pupils only partially develop both Spanish and English abilities. By increasing pupils' capacities in Spanish, he hopes to:

> develop in my pupils the love for the language – to search the
> language – to find the patterns that are in language ... rhyming
> ... alliteration ... *trabalenguas* [tongue twisters] ... to me it's
> fun, to me it's really a way to show that you control the
> language, and I do [develop these skills] with my pupils. (S1)

Teacher S1 used Spanish almost exclusively in literacy and numeracy lessons observed, both in whole- and small-group activities, as well as in discussions with individual pupils.

Teacher S2 was observed using Spanish as the sole medium of instruction in teaching reading, writing, and mathematics. She explains that she also uses Spanish to build background for science and social studies lessons that will later be taught in English. She believes that first-language development is important in creating a foundation that can later be used for English acquisition (S2).

Lessons observed in reading, writing, and mathematics were conducted completely in Spanish in teacher S3's classroom. She believes that first-language development is beneficial for pupils because it builds on their current oral language abilities and it prevents them from becoming overwhelmed by the demands of an all-English classroom.

In contrast to teachers' implementation of the strictly prescribed Literacy Hour at Forest Hill, all four first-grade ESL and bilingual teachers were observed using the Four Blocks model flexibly, both in selection of content and the amount of time spent on a given activity or portion of a lesson. Teacher S1 explains: 'I do [Four Blocks] the way I find it is helpful for my kids', rather than simply following an externally developed plan.

(c) Assessment of ESL/Bilingual Pupils

ESL and bilingual pupils at Shady Ridge complete a variety of assessments, for both LEP-specific and general assessment purposes. Upon arrival, pupils who speak a language other than English at home complete an oral (kindergarten to second grade) or reading (third to fifth grade) proficiency test, either in Spanish or English, depending on their first language. The scores determine pupils' placement in a bilingual, ESL, or mainstream classroom. These tests are then repeated annually for each LEP pupil (S6).

Pupils also take state and national assessments, of which the state assessments are generally considered by staff to be the most important for purposes of individual, school, and district accountability. LEP pupils can be exempted from part or all of the examinations if they do not meet specific language proficiency guidelines (S6). If pupils pass the English portion of the state assessment, they may exit from the ESL or bilingual programme and be placed in a mainstream classroom (S6).

Although the test format and structure is anticipated to change in coming years, many teachers criticize the current state assessments for the following reasons:

- The tests do not reflect pupils' cultures
- They are geared to 'average', white, middle-class pupils
- The Spanish version uses more difficult vocabulary than the English version (S2, 7, 10, 17).

These factors are identified by teachers as disadvantaging LEP pupils specifically and hindering their performance in the state examinations, whether taken in English or Spanish. However, teachers S2 and S6 find that Spanish versions of the assessments have become more linguistically appropriate in recent years.

In first-grade classes, ESL and bilingual teachers assess LEP pupils throughout the year, using evaluation instruments common to all first-grade classrooms, although bilingual teachers use translated versions. Specifically, all pupils are given a state-wide 'reading inventory' three times a year to identify those in need of a compensatory Reading Acceleration Program (RAP), which takes place in the classroom as part of daily literacy instruction (see Appendix L). Additionally, every six weeks teachers are to produce 'running records' of pupils' current achievement of literacy and numeracy benchmarks (S3, 4).

The first-grade teachers' approaches to assessment vary considerably, although all find the classroom and state assessments to be problematic. For example, teacher S4 thinks that the reading inventory is inappropriate for ESL pupils because they do not have the vocabulary and phonemic awareness skills necessary to fully participate in the test. Additionally, she believes that a lack of visual aids in the assessment disadvantages ESL pupils, who tend to rely more heavily on non-verbal stimuli. Teacher S3 finds the Spanish version of the reading inventory is inappropriate because it does not adequately account for the syllabic structure of Spanish.

All first-grade bilingual teachers believe that pupils are subject to too many assessments, none of which they believe adequately reflects their pupils' abilities. Teachers S1 and S2 explain that they try to minimize formal assessment tasks as much as possible. They conduct their 'running records' through observation rather than testing sessions.

5. Factors Affecting Language-in-Education Policy Implementation

(a) School Funding and Institutional Support

The district's ESL/bilingual director, as well as some of the campuses' ESL specialists, believe that the state's language-in-education policies are often based on political agendas rather than language acquisition research (S8, 13). Also, although the director describes the district administration's financial and institutional support for the programme as 'mild', she thinks that there is neither consensus nor broad support district-wide for the ESL/bilingual programme. An ESL specialist from another elementary school in the district explains that an ideal situation would be:

> to have a consistent program, [and] everybody across the district ... knows why we're doing what we're doing, and agrees ... because it's been marketed, publicized, sold, and bought by administrators, teachers, support personnel, families, and students. (S13)

Additionally, funding for the ESL/bilingual programme within each elementary school in the district varies significantly, as a result of the principal's budgetary priorities (S6). This results in broad disparities among cluster schools in the quality of provision they can provide.

The district supports LEP pupils and their teachers through the ESL/bilingual programme office, whose director facilitates coordination between schools and personnel training (S8). Some ESL specialists identify their weekly meetings at the district office as highly beneficial in implementing their campuses' programmes more effectively (S6, 13). Additionally, the district provides ESL and bilingual classroom teachers with specialized training, as well as curricular support through a newly-appointed bilingual reading specialist (S8). However, one first-grade teacher at Shady Ridge is sceptical about the level of involvement or impact the reading specialist will have in her classroom (S2).

Most ESL and bilingual teachers interviewed identify the ESL specialist and each other as valuable resources. Teachers report that the ESL specialist has been beneficial in:

- Obtaining and disseminating materials and strategies
- Advocating their needs at the school and district level
- Translating material into Spanish (S1, 2, 3, 4, 5).

All first-grade teachers report that they rely on each other as sources for pedagogical ideas, curricular materials, and teaching strategies. However, no formal weekly meeting time for the four first-grade ESL/bilingual teachers has been established to facilitate this collaboration.

(b) School Resources

In contrast to Forest Hill, the ESL/bilingual programme at Shady Ridge receives funding that many teachers consider adequate and fairly allocated. As one first-grade teacher explains:

> Funds? ... I don't have a problem with that. You know [the principal] is really giving, and I think that when you have respect for each other, and she knows what you're doing in the classroom ... If you say I need it, you'll get it. It's just that simple. (S2)

Another teacher believes that this situation is the exception rather than the rule for schools in this area: 'I've seen more resources in this school than I've seen teaching in five or six different schools ... This is the strongest [program] I've ever been in' (S7). An office for the ESL specialist and individual classrooms for each of the ESL/bilingual teachers provide physical space for staff to teach and prepare for lessons. Although most ESL teachers do not identify a shortage of planning time as a hindrance to their work, many bilingual teachers wish, as many EMAS staff at Forest Hill do, that they could have more time for making first-language resources (S2, 3, 5, 6).

The teachers in the bilingual programme identify an inequality in the provision of English- and Spanish-language curriculum materials as one of their most pressing problems. While some teachers think the school has greatly improved the quantity of Spanish and other dual-language books available, they explain the selection is still not equivalent to that of the English-medium materials (S1, 2, 3, 4). Also, although district-adopted textbooks are available in Spanish versions, some teachers, particularly those at the upper grades, believe they are too difficult for their pupils to use without significant modifications (S5, 17). Additionally, the Spanish reading books provided in classrooms for bilingual pupils are seen by some teachers as older, fewer, and in worse condition than the reading books in English-medium classrooms (S2, 3, 5, 17).

In some cases, however, adequate bilingual books and curricular resources are simply not available for purchase; therefore, teachers must translate the English curriculum into Spanish as part of their lesson preparation. All bilingual teachers interviewed believe the time required to translate their own materials and create their own Spanish resources is a significant difficulty in teaching LEP pupils. As teacher S3 explains, 'Everything is done for the English teachers, step by step ... but there [is] nothing for us ... we modify everything we need ... it's like doing our job twice.' Additionally, some bilingual teachers in the higher grades believe that there is a shortage of Spanish literature published for this age group (S10, 17). Teacher S10 expresses her frustration: 'How can I "sell" them literature in Spanish? It's not there. We need authors who have [had] their experiences.' Most of what is available is translated from English, and therefore does not adequately reflect pupils' cultures (S10).

(c) Professional Development and Teacher Training

All teachers interviewed at Shady Ridge have received training in the literacy and numeracy programmes used school-wide, but many teachers, like those at Forest Hill, believe these sessions do not address ESL and bilingual issues specifically. The lack of emphasis on LEP pupils' needs within these training sessions appears to contribute to a sense of cynicism among some ESL and bilingual teachers, as teacher S2 explains: 'I don't really understand why we have to go to the English training when a lot of times it doesn't benefit a bilingual teacher ... [The local and regional authorities] really need to develop academies and workshops for bilingual teachers.'

The principal recognizes that ESL and bilingual staff need additional training, and provides frequent opportunities for bilingual teachers to attend specific in-service sessions, in contrast to the 'cascade' method of training at Forest Hill (S6, 11). Shady Ridge's principal hopes her approach will allow teachers to become leaders by 'trying to build that capacity within themselves because ... we want everybody to ... be able to go out, talk about ... and become experts at their craft' (S11). While most teachers identify this training as helpful, one teacher explains that even those sessions focused on bilingual pupils have not been well presented (S2).

Although specific ESL/bilingual in-service training has been provided for LEP teachers, other staff have not had this type of professional development. Mainstream teachers at Shady Ridge do not teach ESL and bilingual pupils, and so they, like teachers at Forest Hill, do not receive specialized training regarding English-language learners. It is quite probable, therefore, that mainstream teachers at Shady Ridge are largely unaware of the needs of LEP pupils, who comprise over one-third of the school.

The internal training that many ESL/bilingual teachers identify as most helpful is not, in fact, language-related. A series of 'building relationships' in-service sessions, designed to help staff communicate more effectively with each other and with pupils, has been provided for all Shady Ridge personnel. Many teachers believe that these sessions have improved both the school environment and professional relationships among staff (S1, 6, 9).

First-grade ESL and bilingual teachers have identified the following as areas in which they would like additional training:

- ESL pupils' first languages and cultures
- ESL teaching strategies
- The incorporation of literature into literacy development
- Reading and writing instruction strategies (S1, 2, 3, 4).

Interestingly, many of these teachers consider collaborative work with colleagues to be one of the most beneficial means of gaining new expertise. ESL teacher S4 explains that she wants 'a really good role model ... I could just watch him or her, and see how they go about teaching and how they work with these kinds of kids, because I learn a lot by observation.' Also, teachers S2 and S3 believe that using each other's expertise can result in better bilingual resources: 'Instead of depending on somebody else to do it, I think whenever you can get a team of teachers to develop something, you probably have better success' (S2).

(d) School Leadership

Most staff interviewed identify the principal as a significant advocate for the ESL/bilingual programme. Many teachers note the principal's positive influence in procuring extra funding, providing training, supporting innovation, and encouraging creativity (S1, 2, 3, 4, 5, 6, 9). Teacher S3 explains that '[the principal] knows she sometimes needs to bend the rules for the bilingual program'; she has adjusted the budget and resources in recognition of the challenges facing bilingual teachers (S3). Additionally, the ESL specialist explains that the principal does not focus heavily on state assessment preparation, thereby reducing the high-pressure testing environment she believes is promoted in other schools. She contends that the principal's focus on developing 'quality instruction' has improved teaching for LEP pupils (S6).

The principal believes that she contributes to the programme by giving ESL and bilingual teachers smaller classes, adequate support staff, and a sizeable budget for the purchase of Spanish materials. Interestingly, bilingual classes in first grade are larger than English-medium ones, and some bilingual teachers think that there are not adequate numbers of classroom assistants (S1, 3, 6).

(e) Professional Relations and the Status of ESL/Bilingual Staff

ESL and bilingual teachers and support staff have daily responsibilities almost identical to those of their mainstream counterparts, in contrast to EMAS staff at Forest Hill. Nonetheless, some teachers at Shady Ridge feel that their roles are not fully understood (S1, 2). One teacher notes that 'teaching kids with other languages is an extra effort that not many people appreciate ... even your own colleagues', but he believes that the 'building relationships' training has helped promote greater understanding among teachers (S1). However, some bilingual teachers believe that they are placed at a professional disadvantage to their colleagues when material resources are provided exclusively for English-medium teachers (S2, 3).

(f) Staffing Allocations

The ESL specialist and the principal identify the school's staffing strategy as a factor that has improved the quality of the ESL and bilingual programmes. The principal explains that her ability to completely re-create her staff after the school's reconstitution allowed her to maximize the number of staff who have bilingual skills and/or the ability to work with LEP pupils (S11). One teacher believes that the principal has been able to 'surround herself [with staff] in this school who are strong in their areas, and they ... share the same goals' (S9). Additionally, the ESL specialist explains that the principal has placed the most skilled bilingual teachers at the lower grades to help improve pupils' foundations in literacy and numeracy (S6).

According to district policy, each bilingual teacher should receive a full-time assistant. Although the district has supplied staffing for this mandate in the past, the allocation has now been reduced (S6). The bilingual programme is currently allotted the equivalent of five-and-a-half assistants for a total of twelve bilingual teachers. First-grade teachers S1 and S3 believe that they were somewhat misled when the district promised them each a full-time assistant when they were hired. They believe that the current level of staffing is not adequate and that a full-time assistant would help them teach more effectively (S1, 3).

Because of the small number of pupils enrolled in the ESL rather than the bilingual programme, ESL teachers are often given non-LEP pupils to equalize class sizes. Some of these ESL teachers would prefer a 'true' ESL class, in which all pupils are acquiring English as a non-native language so that they could focus more fully on pupils' language development (S7, 12). As one second-grade ESL teacher believes, 'If it were truly an ESL class, I could really focus on the [LEP students], but my numbers are getting high now ... it's just a regular class with a lot of "low" kids, and those are hard classes to handle' (S12). In contrast, other ESL teachers find that there is little difference between teaching 'mixed' or all-ESL classes (S4, 5).

(g) Complexities of First-Language Use

Shady Ridge's implementation of a first-language programme highlights the difficulties inherent in introducing bilingual programmes when national policies and trends have historically been assimilationist in nature (Wiley, 2000). Teachers have had varied preparation in Spanish, which has significant consequences for the oral instruction and written translations they must provide. Additionally, pupils' first-language skills differ, as they do at Forest Hill, based upon their previous academic experience and the dialect of the language they speak. Thus, curriculum and resources must be responsive to a wide range of teachers' and pupils' first-language backgrounds.

Many of the bilingual teachers were raised in the United States in non-bilingual school environments themselves. As a result, some of them believe that their spoken and written Spanish skills were underdeveloped (S2, 3, 9, 16). Teaching has forced them, therefore, to improve their vocabulary, writing skills, and general fluency through practice in the classroom.

Unlike bilingual instructors at Forest Hill, Shady Ridge's bilingual teachers must produce extensive written translations in addition to providing oral first-language input during lessons. Translation of the curriculum, already noted as a time-consuming task, must be undertaken by individuals who are not only fluent and literate in Spanish, but also familiar with the specific terminology and technical vocabulary used in that curriculum. In reality, few staff at the school level, other than the teachers themselves, have this level of specialized knowledge; it is these teachers, however, who have such limited time. Also, some of these bi-literate teachers are not confident of their written translation abilities.

Even teacher S17, a Spanish speaker raised in Mexico, worries that her translation skills may not be adequate to prepare pupils for the state assessments; she wonders: 'I mean, am I helping them or am I just ... making it worse?'

Spanish-speaking pupils enter Shady Ridge with a variety of first-language abilities. Most first-grade teachers believe that pupils' relative strengths in English and Spanish vary from individual to individual and from year to year (S1, 2, 3). A general tendency that these teachers note among these pupils, however, is that they have low-level Spanish vocabularies, which some teachers believe to be a result of limited interactions in 'academic' Spanish outside school (S1, 2, 3).

Within a first-language curriculum, the choice of the dialect used for instruction has significant consequences. Although the majority of the Spanish-speaking pupils at Shady Ridge come from Mexico, they and their parents may speak one or more of a multitude of regional dialects. Some teachers believe that pupils predominantly hear and interact in a mixture of Spanish and English common among residents along the state's border with Mexico (S6, 16). Therefore, although pupils are being taught in their 'first language', it may not match the language variety spoken in their home or community.

6. Conclusion

Although LEP pupils represent less than half of Shady Ridge's population, significant efforts are made to support these children's language development through the ESL/bilingual programme. ESL pupils comprise a small percent of Shady Ridge's LEP pupils and do not receive first-language instruction, but full-time ESL instruction is provided by specially trained teachers who are well-supported by the ESL specialist. In the bilingual programme, the use of the late-exit model and the predominance of Spanish-speaking staff create an environment which is very supportive of first-language development. Bilingual teachers and staff, like those at Forest Hill, devote much time and effort to creating bilingual resources; their task is even more complex, however, because Spanish is the primary medium of instruction. Although the ESL/bilingual programme benefits from generous funding and administrative support at the school, a variety of difficulties – political, linguistic, and curricular – demonstrate the challenges inherent in providing effective educational opportunities for pupils from diverse language backgrounds.

CHAPTER 7

Comparative Analysis and Conclusions

Comparison, Bereday's final stage of analysis, necessitates the synthesizing of the two case studies to determine the commonalities in how national, regional, and local authorities, as well as schools, cope with the demands of multi-lingual school populations. Such a comparison, however, must be placed in the context of the two countries' language-in-education policies.

1. Foundations of Language-in-Education Policies

Although the policies of England and the United States have similar goals for their EAL and LEP pupils, the role of the school and community in first-language acquisition is fundamentally different. In both contexts, English-language acquisition is regarded as the most significant outcome of EAL or ESL/bilingual provision. Commenting on the Swann Report in his later *Education for All: a brief guide to the main issues of the Report*, Lord Swann explains that:

> A good command of English is essential to equality of opportunity, academic success, and ... to participation on equal terms as a full member of society. First priority must therefore be given to the learning of English. (Swann, 1985, p. 11)

In the United States, federal legislation also emphasizes the centrality of English-language acquisition. Six of the nine stated purposes of the 'English Language Acquisition, Language Enhancement, and Academic Achievement Act' in *No Child Left Behind* specifically address English acquisition, but none mentions the role of first languages in the language-learning process (US Department of Education, 2001). US states which have bilingual programmes usually dictate that they should operate at the elementary level only and should be transitional in nature, so that upon completion pupils can succeed in English-only environments (Lindholm-Leary, 2001). Thus, the primary educational objective of both countries' policies is the acquisition of English, rather than the maintenance or development of first languages. While these policies may permit the learning of first languages in some circumstances, they do not actively promote such activities at the national level and would be considered only 'toleration-oriented', according to Kloss's (1971) classifications. Both are, therefore, assimilationist in nature, according to Cobarrubias's definition of the term:

> The basic tenet of linguistic assimilation is that all speakers of languages other than the dominant language should be able to speak and function in the dominant language, regardless of their origin. It attaches linguistic superiority to the dominant language ... (1983, pp. 63-64)

This conclusion concerning the policies of England and the United States is consistent with those of Stubbs (1991), Rassool (1995), Harris (1997), Wiley (2000), and Lindholm-Leary (2001).

Although language policies in England and the United States have consistently promoted the primacy of English, the case study research revealed that school environments have become more accepting of the presence of first languages. The head teacher at Forest Hill explains that the school currently encourages pupils to speak their first languages informally. This approach is:

> a huge change, because [in the past] they weren't allowed to speak in their home language. You walked through the door and you spoke English or you didn't speak; it was as simple as that. (F4)

Additionally, at Shady Ridge, some teachers recall that bilingual education was not available when they attended school. For example, teacher S12, a native Spanish speaker, was placed in an all-English immersion class when she attended elementary school, and she explains, 'I wish we had back then [the bilingual program] we have now.'

Policy documents in England and the United States support the notion that first-language competence is beneficial to second-language learning, but the responsibility for first-language acquisition is assumed by different groups in the two countries. In England, national policy recommendations state that it is the primary responsibility of the community, rather than the school, to provide this first-language instruction. According to the Swann Report:

> We would regard mother tongue maintenance, although an important educational function, as best achieved within ethnic minority communities themselves rather than within mainstream schools ... (Committee of Inquiry into the Education of Children from Ethnic Minority Groups, 1985, p. 406)

Thus, as Brumfit (1995) explains, 'lingualism', meaning language development, is undertaken by schools only in English, while 'multi-lingualism', including first-language acquisition and maintenance, is the responsibility of the community. In the United States, however, national policies do not preclude a state education agency, such as that in Texas, from assuming responsibility for teaching first-language skills, at least at the elementary level.

The roles of schools in facilitating cultural and linguistic acquisition also differ in the two countries. In England, policy recommendations emphasize the school's responsibility to assist EAL pupils in achieving a *cultural* acquisition through maximizing their integration with mainstream pupils. The Swann Report states, 'We believe that any form of separate provision catering exclusively for ethnic minority pupils serves to establish and confirm social divisions between groups of pupils' (Committee of Inquiry, 1985, pp. 406-407). In the United States, national policies, although allowing significant freedom to states and districts, retain a stronger focus on schools' need to facilitate the *language* acquisition of LEP pupils, even if this must be achieved through separate provision and at the expense of immediate cultural integration. Such an emphasis can be perceived in the federal requirement that LEP pupils' English-language ability be tested nation-wide and that schools should be accountable for annual improvement (US Department of Education, 2001).

2. Characteristics of National and State Policies

Despite similar assimilationist foci, national language-in-education policies in England and the United States differ in several aspects, including the extent of their statutory authority and their subsequent interpretation; the manner in which they address EAL or LEP pupils' needs in the curriculum; and the professional status which they afford the teachers of these individuals.

EAL policies in England are determined through national *recommendations* rather than national legislation; in the United States, on the other hand, English-language learners are addressed directly in federal education acts, as well as in judicial decisions. National guidance in both countries is then interpreted locally, at the LEA and school level in England, and at the state, district, and school level in the United States. It is significant to note that states and districts in the US appear to have broader powers of interpretation than LEAs or schools in England. Thus, it is possible for submersion, transitional bilingual, and two-way bilingual programmes to co-exist in one US state or district. In contrast, all English LEAs and schools are *recommended* to follow the submersion model, in which pupils participate in mainstream English-medium classes with first-language support to enable access to the curriculum.

The extent to which English-language learners' needs are addressed in curricula is a significant manifestation of language-in-education policies. Although England has a National Curriculum, no distinct guidelines for EAL pupils are outlined therein. No separate EAL curriculum has been established, a fact which Cable & Leung (1997) believe has contributed to the 'marginalized status of English as an additional language within mainstream educational provision' (p. 2). In the United States, no national curriculum exists, and it is therefore the states' prerogative to establish their own. Notably, Texas has developed curriculum standards for Spanish language arts and English as a second language at the primary level.

Finally, the professional status of teachers serving EAL and LEP pupils is dependent to some degree upon the existence of discipline-specific training and qualifications. In England, no professional qualification is required for employment as an EMAS teacher or bilingual instructor, although some LEAs may prefer individuals with particular training or experience. However, states in the US are able to dictate their own teacher certification criteria, and many offer qualifications in ESL and/or bilingual education as specializations within initial teacher training. As Leung (2001) notes, the availability of recognized training increases the credibility of an EAL or ESL/bilingual teacher among other staff.

3. Factors Affecting Policy Implementation

Although language-in-education policies in the two countries are distinct, the case studies reveal certain common factors which affect their implementation. As discussed in Chapter Two, both Miedema (1997) and Cardinale et al (1999) have completed investigations revealing the difficulties involved in putting such policies into action. The efforts of schools in Miedema's study are circumscribed by societal pressures, assessment pressures, and external circumstances which limit schools' priorities and resources. The work of Cardinale et al, however, finds that the issues complicating bilingual education at the district level include logistical demands, teacher recruitment, 'politicization', race relations, and community support. These two studies represent significantly different educational situations; nevertheless, it is still possible to relate the issues they discuss to one of the following general categories: *internal* pressures resulting from scarce resources, and *societal and political* pressures. While the complexity of education in multi-lingual situations cannot be reduced to such a simple dichotomy, this differentiation is a useful tool in analysing the findings of the current study in light of previous research.

The manner in which language-in-education policies are implemented at Forest Hill (England) and Shady Ridge (United States) highlights the complications encountered in providing effective services for EAL and LEP pupils. Such issues relate to:

- *Internal* pressures resulting from scarce resources: school funding, teacher training, and staffing allocations
- *Societal and political* pressures: programme instability, professional relations, school leadership, and the complexities of first-language use.

Both schools benefit from extra funding specifically targeted for EAL and ESL/bilingual staff and/or resources. Additionally, the head teacher and principal are both given a degree of freedom in the specific management of their budgets. When management places a high priority on these programmes, as is the case at Shady Ridge, this flexibility benefits teachers and pupils through the provision of personnel and resources. However, when other priorities, such as the recent construction programme at Forest Hill, restrict the budget, the ability of staff to address EAL/LEP concerns is hindered by a lack of resources.

Initiatives undertaken by teachers and instructors in both schools have the potential to greatly increase the quantity and quality of curricular and other resources available to EAL/LEP teachers and their pupils. Forest Hill teachers' action research and the subsequent efforts of the literacy working group have led to the ongoing development of a literacy strategy more appropriate for English-language learners. At Shady Ridge, first-grade teachers' development of a Spanish-language literacy curriculum also demonstrates significant commitment to creating more relevant and effective teaching and learning materials. In the two schools, teachers and assistants also show a willingness to create multi-lingual resources when none exist. Translating substantial portions of the curriculum (as Shady Ridge's bilingual teachers must do) contributes to teachers' workload considerably. Although the ESL specialist assists with these tasks, teachers explain that translating still demands much of their time. Forest Hill EMAS staff do not need to create multi-lingual resources on such an expansive scale; nonetheless, they are hindered by a lack of physical space and coordination time. In both cases, it would be beneficial to increase the time teachers and other staff can spend in mutual collaboration with each other to build upon their strengths and burgeoning expertise.

Specialized in-service training is available for personnel in both schools, although the impact of this training affects the schools differently. Members of EMAS and ESL/bilingual staff have multiple opportunities to develop their knowledge of language acquisition issues, through training at the LEA/district or regional level. In contrast, these schools do not have the resources to provide all mainstream teachers in these settings with such in-service experiences. Because initial teacher training in both countries usually does not require a basic knowledge of

EAL or ESL/bilingual issues, these teachers often have little awareness of the challenges facing English-language learners. In Shady Ridge classrooms, LEP pupils receive most of their academic instruction from a certified ESL or bilingual teacher who has continuing access to training, but at Forest Hill this situation appears to be more problematic. EAL pupils spend the vast majority of their time with mainstream teachers, rather than EMAS staff.

At both sites, school administrators have been successful in maintaining a measure of control over staffing arrangements. The schools have recently experienced administrative changes – an amalgamation of two schools in one case and a complete staffing reconstitution in the other – which have allowed the head teacher and principal to determine their teaching and support personnel to a greater degree than at many schools. Additionally, the head teacher at Forest Hill has been able to influence recent EMAS staffing changes and hire a temporary bilingual instructor. Despite these efforts, teachers in the two schools believe that additional bilingual support personnel are still needed in classes with English-language learners. While some Shady Ridge bilingual teachers simply wish for a full-time, rather than a shared, assistant in their classes, Forest Hill's staffing shortage appears more complicated. As the school's EMAS coordinator explains:

> It's very difficult to get the access you need, and for 500
> children with a second language there are just three of us full-
> time and three of us part-time. It's just not possible [to help
> everyone]. (F1)

Such difficulties limit the extent to which EMAS staff can provide support to individual pupils on a regular basis, especially when pressure exists to prepare pupils for SATs in years two and six.

Societal and political pressures also affect the manner in which language-in-education policies are implemented. LEA and district authorities in both case studies are concerned with the instability of their EAL/LEP programmes and the possible deleterious effects future changes may have. In England, the prospect of annual changes in funding, a result of political decisions or changing numbers of pupils, causes insecurity. This instability has the potential to restrict the efforts of administrators and instructors, who are unsure as to whether their positions will be available in coming years. Such a situation could contribute to the widespread shortage of qualified EMAS staff in England (OFSTED, 1999; Leung, 2001). Administrators and teachers in Shady Ridge's district, however, are more concerned about changes in *policy*, rather than funding. They are worried that LEP programmes' organization and content will have to be significantly altered because of changes in governmental directives which do not adequately consider the needs of LEP pupils.

Both schools have undertaken efforts to integrate EMAS and ESL/bilingual personnel into the school community as a whole. Some teachers at Forest Hill have begun to incorporate bilingual staff more directly into the delivery of their lessons. Although the EMAS coordinator plans to expand such initiatives, these efforts could be hindered by the lack of common planning time currently available in the school timetable. At Shady Ridge, training in interpersonal skills has helped to facilitate communication between ESL/bilingual and mainstream teachers, who meet together at their grade level on a weekly basis. Purposeful and integrated whole-staff development and coordination, then, are vital to create and maintain successful programmes. Berman et al (1995) found that those schools which provide 'exemplary learning environments' for LEP pupils have undertaken reform and reorganization on a *school-wide* basis (cited in Mohan et al, 2001, p. 219).

Rampton (1990) emphasizes the need to perceive EAL/LEP pupils as possessors of 'dynamic ethnicities', unique in their language expertise, affiliations, and traditions. This linguistic complexity, when compounded by the diversity of languages present in the two case-study schools, offers significant challenges in attempting to address the language needs of *all* pupils. Pupils whose first languages are spoken by just a few individuals – such as the Malay speakers at Forest Hill or the Hindi speaker at Shady Ridge – are much less likely to receive first-language support at any school (Corson, 1991). For those languages spoken by a significant number of pupils, all first-language provision is affected by variations in instructors' and pupils' dialects and literacy skills. These complications are more significant in Shady Ridge's bilingual programmes, in which Spanish is used as the spoken *and* written medium of instruction. Thus, teachers and administrators at the school and LEA/district levels should ensure that first-language provision is consistent among instructors and instructional materials. Such a commitment to provide the most effective and responsive language support requires that programmes for EAL and LEP pupils become a financial and political priority.

4. Conclusion

Linguistic and cultural diversity, rather than homogeneity, is a reality for schools in England and the United States, despite the largely assimilationist rhetoric of national language policies. Kaplan & Baldauf (1997) contend that 'the notion of the existence of a "standard" [language] variety ... suggests a level of ... unity which is entirely contrary to the reality of linguistic diversity' (p. 123). The extent to which policies allow for the maintenance and development of minority language pupils' cultural and linguistic knowledge is becoming an increasingly important issue in both countries. This study has analysed both the rhetoric of national policies and their implementation at a local level to evaluate the extent to which EAL/LEP pupils' language needs are addressed at the primary school level.

Significantly, the case study research has revealed that individual schools and teachers have recognized EAL/LEP pupils' first-language needs to a greater extent than that required by national policies. Although the medium of curriculum delivery and assessment at Forest Hill is English, first languages and native cultures are widely valued. More importantly, however, the EMAS staff, some teachers, and senior management support the development of more linguistically appropriate curriculum and the use of bilingual instruction in an increasing number of contexts. While bilingual education is mandated at Shady Ridge, the schools' teachers have developed a new bilingual curriculum, and the administration supports a late-exit bilingual programme model (unlike other schools in the district), which gives pupils additional years of instructional time in their first language.

The presentation of these two case studies in a comparative context 'directs us to search out and try to understand forces and factors at work that transcend ... boundaries' (Noah, 1986, p. 155). Qualitative research methods have provided the 'thick description' and insights necessary to understand these particular school environments, their commonalities, and their differences.

Internal pressures, resulting from scarce resources, have affected the nature and extent of provision, as both schools attempt to meet the academic and linguistic needs of their EAL/LEP pupils. Teachers in the two schools would benefit from additional collaborative sessions and joint planning time to build upon existing knowledge and materials. To make such an endeavour truly beneficial, however, it would also be necessary for Forest Hill to devote additional resources to instructional materials and staffing which directly impact on the education of linguistic minorities.

Societal and political pressures also affect policy implementation in both schools. The possibilities of policy and funding changes threaten the ability of these programmes to maintain their current levels of support for EAL/LEP pupils. Additionally, all staff members in the schools would benefit from a greater awareness of the responsibilities, challenges, and complexity inherent in teaching minority language pupils, in their first languages or in English. Although Forest Hill Primary and Shady Ridge Elementary cannot be seen as necessarily representative of their national or local contexts, they are nonetheless indicative of Kaplan & Baldauf's 'reality of linguistic diversity'. Policy implementation difficulties and successes in these situations, therefore, are pertinent to broader discussions of multi-lingual education.

Appendices

APPENDIX A
Classification of Language-in-Education Programmes

Baker & Jones (1998) outline a range of language-in-education programmes, for both minority and majority language speakers, which they have divided into 'weak' and 'strong' forms of bilingual education. Most programmes in the United States and England for English-language learners are considered submersion, or at best, transitional programmes. Maintenance programmes for minority language pupils are the most highly recommended in language acquisition research, and some programmes with these aims can be found at the primary level in the United States. Multi-lingual education is not addressed in this classification.

'Minority language' refers to any language spoken by a minority of the population that does not have national or official status. 'Majority language' refers to the official, national, or dominant language that is spoken by the majority of the population, such as English in the United States and England. 'L1' refers to a student's first spoken language, and 'L2' refers to an additional language the student then acquires.

Type of programme	Type of child	Language of the classroom	Societal and educational aim	Aim in language outcome
Weak forms of education for bilingualism				
1. *Submersion* (structured immersion)	Language minority	Majority language	Assimilation	Monolingualism
2. *Submersion* (withdrawal classes/sheltered English)	Language minority	Majority language with 'pull-out' lessons	Assimilation	Monolingualism
3. *Segregationist*	Language minority	Minority language (forced, no choice)	Apartheid	Monolingualism

4. *Transitional*	Language minority	Moves from minority to majority language	Assimilation	Relative monolingualism
5. *Mainstream* (with foreign language teaching)	Language majority	Majority language with L2/FL lessons	Limited enrichment	Limited bilingualism
6. *Separatist*	Language majority	Minority language (out of choice)	Detachment/ autonomy	Limited bilingualism

Strong forms of education for bilingualism

7. *Immersion*	Language majority	Bilingual with initial emphasis on L2	Pluralism and enrichment	Bilingualism and biliteracy
8. *Maintenance/ heritage*	Language minority	Bilingual with emphasis on L1	Maintenance, pluralism and enrichment	Bilingualism and biliteracy
9. *Two-way/ language*	Mixed	Minority and majority	Maintenance, pluralism and enrichment	Bilingualism and biliteracy
10. *Mainstream bilingual*	Language majority	Two majority languages	Maintenance, pluralism and enrichment	Bilingualism and biliteracy

Table AI. Classification of language-in-education programmes.

APPENDIX B
England's School Structure and Assessment System

Year	Age	
Reception	4-5	
1	5-6	Key Stage 1
2	6-7	
3	7-8	
4	8-9	Key Stage 2
5	9-10	
6	10-11	
7	11-12	
8	12-13	Key Stage 3
9	13-14	
10	14-15	Key Stage 4
11	15-16	
12	16-17	
13	17-18	

Table AII. English school year and assessment structures.

Students participate in the following national assessments:

Tests
Reading/writing/spelling: age 7, 11
Mathematics: age 7, 11, 14
Mental arithmetic: age 11, 14
Science: age 11, 14
English: age 14

Teacher Assessments
Mathematics: age 7, 11, 14
English: age 7, 11, 14
Science: age 7, 11, 14
History: age 14
Geography: age 14
Modern foreign language: age 14
Design and technology: age 14
Information technology: age 14
Art: age 14
Music: age 14
PE: age 14

For more information, see DfES (2003b).

APPENDIX C
'Standard English' in English:
the National Curriculum for England

The National Curriculum for English (DfEE, 1999b) includes the teaching of 'standard English' from Key Stage 1 through Key Stage 4. With regard to the use of language, the National Curriculum states that:

> Pupils should be taught in all subjects to express themselves correctly and appropriately and to read accurately and with understanding. *Since standard English, spoken and written, is the predominant language in which knowledge and skills are taught and learned*, pupils should be taught to recognise and use standard English. (p. 51, my emphasis)

Many critics disagree with this assertion, claiming that 'even so-called native speakers do not necessarily use standard forms' and that the idea of a single standard English does not recognize modern language use within or across ethnic and linguistic communities, even in formal situations (Leung et al, 1997).

APPENDIX D
National Literacy Strategy

The following extract is from the website of the Department for Education and Skills, explaining the National Literacy Strategy (DfES, 2000).

> *1. What is the national literacy target?*
> The national literacy target is that by 2002, 80% of all 11 year olds will reach the standard expected for their age in English, i.e. level 4 in the Key Stage 2 National Curriculum tests.

> *2. What happens in the Literacy Hour?*
> The daily Literacy Hour has four elements:

> – it starts with the whole class working on a *shared text* where the teacher is able to model effective reading or writing and where all pupils can actively participate;
> – then comes a short period of *word level* or *sentence level* work; for younger children, this will often be used to teach and consolidate phonic knowledge which they can apply in their reading and writing, whereas older pupils might focus more on spelling or sentence construction;

– there is time for *independent work* where pupils apply their literacy skills in meaningful tasks individually, in pairs or in groups; at the same time, the teacher works with small groups to improve specific skills through *guided reading or writing*;
– the final *plenary* session allows teachers and children to reflect on and assess what has been learnt and to think about next steps.

APPENDIX E
Forest Hill Primary: interviewee information

F1 is the Ethnic Minority Achievement Service (EMAS) Coordinator at Forest Hill. After working as a mainstream classroom teacher for seven years, she earned an RSA (Royal Society for the Encouragement of Arts, Manufactures and Commerce) qualification for teaching English as an additional language. She has worked as an EMAS support teacher in both secondary and primary schools in the area. This is her first coordinator position, which she began in September 2002. She is also a member of the school's literacy working group.

F2 is an Arabic speaker from Syria who is employed as a bilingual instructor. She has worked at Forest Hill for three years, although this is her first year full-time. Before this year, her time was divided among several schools in this same urban area throughout the week.

F3 is a year-two classroom teacher. This is her eighth year teaching, although it is only her second at Forest Hill. All of her teaching has taken place in the same urban area, at 'similar schools': those with a somewhat transitory population and a majority of pupils with English as an additional language and/or multi-cultural backgrounds. She is currently the curriculum coordinator for English and Key Stage One. She has received extensive training on the National Literacy Strategy and is a member of Forest Hill's literacy working group.

F4 is the head teacher of Forest Hill. She has worked as a classroom teacher, a department head, and a deputy head at several primary and infant schools in this urban area. When serving as the head teacher of the Forest Hill Infants School, she was asked by the governing body to assume leadership for the amalgamated Forest Hill Primary School in 1997.

F5 is an Urdu/Punjabi speaker who is employed as a bilingual instructor. She has remained in this role for eight years at Forest Hill.

F6 is a year-two classroom teacher. This is her first year teaching after her initial teacher training, which took place at a nearby university.

F7 is the deputy head of service for the city's Ethnic Minority Achievement Service. Originally an English teacher in the city, he has worked on 'remedial', special needs, multi-cultural, and anti-racist advisory councils. He has been involved in EMAS as well as its forerunners: the Language and Learning and Numeracy Support Services, and the Language and Literacy Support Service.

F8 is the school's special needs coordinator. She and another colleague undertook the teacher research into EAL pupils' written errors, the results of which have been used by the literacy working group.

F9 is an Urdu/Punjabi speaker who is employed as an EMAS nursery nurse. Her position focuses on supporting children in the 'early years' at Forest Hill.

F10 is an EMAS (qualified) support teacher who works at Forest Hill three days per week. This is her first year at the school, as well as her first opportunity to work with primary-level pupils. She is a monolingual English speaker.

APPENDIX F
Forest Hill Primary: language demographics

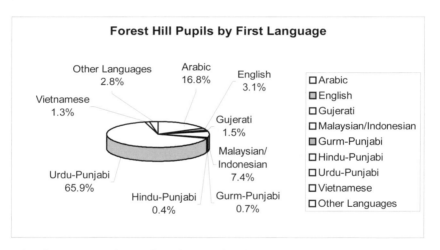

*The three types of Punjabi relate to the different scripts in which they are written: Urdu, Gurmukhi, and Hindu.

Figure A1. Forest Hill pupils by first language (pupils: 457 total).

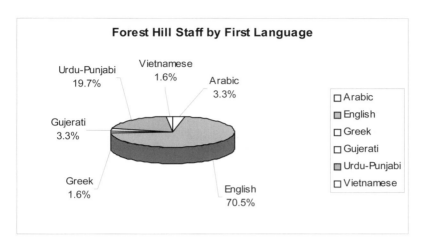

Figure A2. Forest Hill staff by first language (staff: 61 total).

APPENDIX G
Forest Hill Primary: year two classroom language demographics

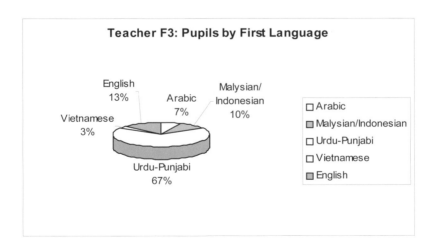

Figure A3. Teacher F3: pupils by first language (Teacher 3: 30 pupils total).

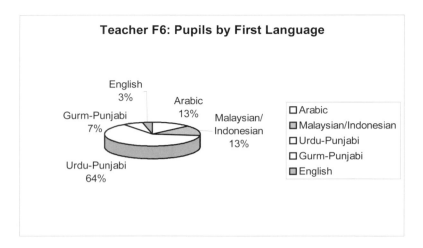

Figure A4. Teacher F6: pupils by first language (Teacher 6: 30 pupils total).

APPENDIX H
Extracts from Taped Interviews: Forest Hill

The following extracts from the taped interviews with Forest Hill and LEA staff are a selection of the quotations referred to, but not included in, Chapter Five. In addition, more information has been gleaned from untaped interviews with teachers and staff at the school.

1. Pupil and Community Characteristics

Transitory nature of Forest Hill families:

> [Arabic speakers are] a transient population and they're only here for three years. (F4)

Impact of community schools:

> That cuts into [your English-language learning] if you're doing the full day here and three hours a night [at the mosque] for five evenings a week. (F1)

> So you can see that although [Arabic parents are] quite supportive, they're not particularly worried about their children's achievement in school. If they learn some English,

it's a bonus, because higher education is done in English [but] basically, Arabic education is more important. (F1)

I also have a theory which could be totally wrong, but if you're reading the Koran [at the mosque] in a language you don't understand, you're not questioning what you read, you're not understanding what you read ... Then [at school] we present them with a text and we say, well, 'Why aren't they very good at inference?' Because they look at the word and they can tell you the word, but the other, deeper skills aren't being accessed, maybe. (F1)

I think ... they work so hard in the day [and are] really pushed all the time with literacy and numeracy ... and I just think it would be so nice just to let them, you know, socialize a bit, because I know they go straight from here to the mosque, a lot of them do. I feel a bit sorry for them sometimes, because they're only kids. (F6)

Role of the Ethnic Minority Achievement Service in community schools:

Before very long [minority groups] start setting up their own schools, usually to enhance their culture, their music, their dance ... and their language, and other cultural aspects. But for the newer groups, the Asian groups, it also includes their religion, so we get a lot of Koranic schools. Now we've supported those, through a small grant, only a couple hundred pounds, and we have a member of staff who goes around and acts as a liaison. (F7)

We made a policy decision that community schools play a very important role in the attainment of our children. We feel they do, because they involve the community, they involve the parents, the children ... they're getting their first language, which is helping this deficit of first language. It's also giving them a lot of self-esteem and self-confidence and pride in themselves. (F7)

Factors affecting parents' participation in the school community:

[Parents do not participate] mainly because ... maybe they don't feel quite so confident in their own abilities, so they don't come to schools because they feel that they wouldn't understand what was going on. (F3)

[The pupils] don't bring a lot of worldly experience, but they bring so much respect. The culture of respect [is] in fact, too [great] at times with the parents; you really have to break down those barriers. It's quite a challenge ... [There is] too much respect in that the parents see, 'That's the school, and we don't come in.' We've got to get the parents to come in, but it's a slow process. It's taken eleven years of breaking down those barriers, and even now when new parents arrive ... they feel quite scared because it's different to their home countries. (F4)

I'd really like to get the parents involved a lot more. I'm not sure how ... I've heard before I started here that a lot of the parents don't feel that they know anything, and I'm sure that they know a lot ... I got told that a lot of the parents don't feel confident enough to work with the children. (F6)

2. Recent Reorganizations and Changes

Funding restrictions resulting from construction of new building:

In terms of the PFI (Pathfinders' privately financed initiative), it's like a mortgage. We're paying for this school, the Council are paying for this school, for the next twenty-five years, so they take a huge wedge of my budget out ... I have less money now, in terms of flexibility, flexible money ... a lot of my money is taken off me at the outset now. (F4)

3. EMAS Staff and Policy

Little conception of a consistent EAL policy:

There's no policy, as such, it's just expected that you respond to the make-up of your school. I don't know what happens in history, geography, science ... how far they take account of the different ethnic heritage there. I think ... it doesn't seem to be addressed as a whole school, this idea of appreciating children's cultures, and I find that staff don't have a knowledge of, for example, the Muslim culture, when 99% of the children are Muslim. That shocked me a little bit because that should be dealt with by the school, I would have thought, years ago because it's been like this for some time now. (F1)

I would say that there is not a policy as such. We monitor results in the schools and we monitor by ethnic group. The policy that we pursue is through our training with our staff ... We monitor the results, and if the results are showing badly for certain groups, we go in and ask the head teachers why ...

and what are you doing about it. Our policy as a whole is that our staff who have this additional training work with teachers in the classroom and thereby train the teachers on the job. (F7)

Curricular concerns as the responsibility of the specific school, not EMAS:

[Curriculum development should] be done in individual schools with individual staff contributing at the planning stage. This is where the partnership comes in. We don't believe ... we can really play that role. (F7)

Role and responsibilities of EMAS staff in delivering policy:

EMAS coordinator's role: The head's agreed that I ... make the time to do all these new things ... We're trying to change the literacy hour, it's one of the initiatives ... In the rest of my time, she's quite happy for me not to be in class but to work on the things which really impact all the pupils. (F1)

The main ways of [supporting pupils are] working and planning with the ... teacher so that the methodology and the content is appropriate, and when you've been doing this job for so long, you can almost foresee ... what's going to cause the problem, what vocabulary or tasks are going to cause a problem. So it's collaborating with teachers and working with the pupils and providing resources if required. (F1)

4. Implementation of Language-in-Education Policies for Non-Native English Speakers

(a) English language development and literacy.

Teachers' and administrators' attitudes regarding the National Literacy Strategy:

I have prioritized what I think are the main weaknesses that appear ... there's not enough time for speaking and listening [and the teaching of grammar rules]. (F1)

[We need to be] focusing on teaching English grammar in a more formal way than we do at the moment ... I don't think there's enough at the sentence level in the strategy for us ... I think we should concentrate more on sentence level work and actually ... teach English as a foreign language because we don't do that at the moment. (F3)

I don't think we focus enough on teaching that grammar; I think it's more incidental. (F3)

First of all, you have to realize that [a grammatical element [is] not there in order to put it in, and I think with a lot of teachers trying to juggle everything else, they're not going to sit down and study [the strategy] at great length and say, 'Right, this is what's missing, this is what I need to do,' because without being told, it's hard to pick up on things like that. (F3)

[We are] looking at the Literacy Strategy ... picking bits out and saying, right, this isn't appropriate for our pupils, let's put in some alternatives. (F4)

[I think the EMAS staff wants to] move away from the literacy strategy and think of their own strategies because of how it's not working due to the SATs results – apparently it's not working. (F6)

Progress of the literacy working group:

We're trying to change the literacy hour; it's one of the initiatives, so we're going to trial those as an experiment. (F1) [We are] going to make the teaching of ... grammar rules specific as part of the literacy hour. (F1)

We're also looking at a project for the summer term, a raising achievement project where ... the English working party [is] going through the [literacy] strategy and putting extra of the most relevant ... teaching in there. And we're going to experiment with a couple of year groups on that. (F4)

(b) First-language development and literacy.

Enthusiasm for simultaneous translation:

Another thing I'm trying to get is a lot more simultaneous translation in class because [there are enough] classroom assistants who belong to the school, not EMAS ... who speak Urdu as their first language to have one in every year of the school. (F1)

Teacher appreciation of the full-time Arabic bilingual instructor:

She's so in demand ... One Arabic-speaking member of staff is not enough. (F3)

When I first started at Forest Hill, there was a lower percentage of Arabic pupils, much lower ... now there's a huge need [for Arabic bilingual instructors]. (F4)

I had an Arabic interpreter for one maths lesson, which was good, but she has to spread herself throughout the whole school ... so she's really busy, and I think she has to concentrate more on the juniors. (F6)

School-wide initiatives to incorporate pupils' first languages are largely restricted to non-curricular activities:

[We incorporate pupils' home cultures] through extracurricular clubs like the dance club and things like that. Maybe the music club, the choir will sing some songs from their countries and things. We do it through displays, through multi-lingual signage, through appointing bilingual staff. (F4)

[Teacher F3] just helps me immensely ... especially to do with that ... Eid celebration we did. (F6)

They say hello [in their language] for the register and good morning and that kind of thing. They like to dance and sing their songs. (F6)

Written translations:

[Bilingual EMAS staff] do a lot of written translation. People need signs and worksheets bilingualized. They'll be in great demand when children do their SATs to translate science and maths papers. (F1)

A proposed Urdu language class for pupils:

[We were] going to sit down and make a program to deliver Urdu lessons at lunchtime two half-hours a week, and the governors have stopped it ... they thought that the children would be too stressed if they worked all morning and all afternoon and had lessons at lunchtime as well. (F1)

We're looking at the moment at introducing Urdu, an Urdu club for speaking Urdu, but I need to talk to governors in detail about that. (F4)

Teacher F3's use of bilingual support:

[Using simultaneous translation] wasn't something I ever saw anybody else doing, and I just didn't think it would work, and then I started doing it with [a non-EMAS bilingual staff

89

member]. It was after a meeting we had. And that was a real eye-opener for me ... and I don't know why I haven't done it [before], and now thinking back on it, it seems the most obvious thing to do. (F3)

[Bilingual support], I think, is invaluable ... [The pupils] so desperately need it. You see they're trying so hard to understand everything that you say, but I can't begin to imagine what it's like for them. (F3)

Teacher F6's use of bilingual support (referring to her full-time Urdu-speaking assistant):

She supports special needs really; she doesn't really support them with the language. (F6)

She interprets at parent evenings. (F6)

I think ... in science ... and maths she's going to start interpreting the main points, I think, she said, but just not yet. (F6)

I've not really had much contact [with EMAS staff]. I don't think we get much contact ... I think it's more [focused on] the juniors. (F6)

(c) Assessment of EAL pupils.

How assessment affects the allocation of EMAS staff:

You've got to look at your SATs results, which are important; league tables are there. We will be ... OFSTEDed, we will be looked at according to our SATs results. They're low; they were very low in 2002. They've increased, but they dipped in 2002 ... but because of that, maybe I'm putting more EMAS staff in at my year two and my year six than I would normally ... I don't think there is any right or wrong answer. I know it's wrong to spread right the way across because they just get too thin on the ground; they don't have enough impact. (F4)

Belief that the national assessments specifically disadvantage EAL pupils:

There is no test in this country for children who speak English as a second language ... I can't see where there can be one really, because everyone is at different levels and they're all coming from different backgrounds anyway ... A non-verbal reasoning test [would be preferable] because [it is] one of the things that highlights[s] underachievement [so if a child] had a high non-verbal reasoning and a low English SAT, you'd think, this child [has] obviously got ability, so something's wrong. (F1)

Frustration that Forest Hill's assessment scores are still measured against those of a 'normative' population:

I feel passionately, really, that the children should be given the opportunity to achieve. And I feel very concerned about the fact that they are measured on the same baseline and that the benchmarking in terms of assessment is based on free school meals and is not based on ethnic minority. So nobody collects information [about] schools with Pakistani children across the country ... and how they compare. That information is not there. (F4)

We need greater understanding from the government about the challenges and about ... how wonderful our children are ... Why should they be measured against English-speaking children? As long as we're showing high expectations and we're raising attainment, then why should it be measured alongside? (F4)

Translations of 'optional' SATs assessments:

[For] the optional assessments ... at years three, four, and five, we've never used bilingual help for that, just because it's such a timetabling nightmare. If you're using all your bilingual help for your testing, then the teaching's not going on, and you can really see the difference. (F4)

Testing pupils according to STEP:

We only do [STEPs assessments] once a year. It used to be twice a year, but it takes us in theory two weeks; we come out of lessons for two weeks to do it, but ... it takes more than that, really. And so to do that twice a year was missing a month out of the classroom. (F1)

As it's only aimed to provide funding, it's a limited tool ... It needs to be incorporated into the other assessments going on to give a full picture, I think. (F1)

EMAS staff attitudes towards half-termly records:

We are supposedly keeping half-termly records, but it always gets pushed to the bottom because there's too much to do. (F1)

Year-two teacher attitudes to Key Stage Two SATs:

> I'm aware of what they need to know by May, so ... the pace of
> my teaching might be different in terms of ... where they are.
> (F3)

> [The sample test questions] gave me a heart attack. I was so
> worried ... [The pupils] are just not up to the standards at all.
> (F6)

> The comprehension's hard as well, I think ... the standards of
> the books and the reading ... it's really tricky. And the way [the
> questions are] phrased ... is tricky. (F6)

> I think [the test format] is the trouble – if I say it in a different
> way, a lot of them will get it ... but just to read the question ...
> that's really hard. (F6)

5. Factors Affecting Language-in-Education Policy Implementation

(a) School funding and institutional support.

Growing concern over EMAS funding:

> I know that on the ground level ... heads and governing bodies
> will have to make some hard decisions and I don't think it will
> be necessarily ring-fenced, which concerns me that our EAL
> pupils could miss out ... I could see in a couple of years' time,
> hard decisions having to be made. For instance ... can we run
> our additional literacy booster classes or do we appoint an
> EMAS teacher? (F4)

> Again, we're not sure what government policy will be. We
> suspect that they might actually try to remove this particular
> funding stream and incorporate it into some more general
> funding stream ... so that's our worry. (F7)

Problematic nature of EMAS funding devolvement:

> [The Service] can take us out of here if they want to because
> we essentially belong to EMAS rather than the school ... but
> generally speaking, if people are working well in the school,
> then you want to keep continuity. (F1)

> Schools are becoming more and more independent [but] that
> means that some schools are going to go awry ... and the
> support mechanisms might not be there from the local

authority ... [It] gives us an interesting dilemma, because the money is with the schools. (F7)

(b) School resources/

Hindrances to the provision of adequate multi-lingual resources:

> There are a few [dual language texts]; I bought some, but it's a drop in the ocean. (F1)

> Well, one thousand pounds is not going to buy enough books ... I've already spent about three hundred of it, and you could put it in a plastic box ... As I said I would like lots more bilingual books and dictionaries in every classroom, and artifacts ... loads of images, and Urdu and Arabic software for translating, CD-ROMs that children can use, like talking books ... lots of things. (F1)

> Especially with multi-cultural resources, books and maps and things like that, we haven't got [much]. We are quite poorly resourced. (F3)

Production of resources by EMAS staff:

> I think as a team we could produce a lot which would be useful in school, but I can't get in the room so I can't get to the computer, and we can't get together, and we don't have a base. (F1)

(c) Professional development and teacher training.

Head teacher philosophy:

> Because we've got such a big staff, I do encourage them to cascade the training down, so I may only send one member of staff from that year group and they need to cascade to the other[s]. (F4)

EMAS staff responses to training provided by the Service:

> Like any training, it depends on the person who's delivering the training. Some of it's very good and some isn't ... A lot of it in the past has been we discuss a topic, the trainer writes it on the flipchart and regurgitates it back, so in other words we're taking our own knowledge and having it fed back to us, and I don't think that's training ... but more and more they're getting in experts ... so it is improving. (F1)

Lack of specific EAL training for mainstream teachers:

> It's just a mixed batch, because ... these sorts of [EAL] issues aren't included in people's initial teacher training ... It's just constantly getting through people's ignorance about the role [of EMAS] and the children's needs. (F1)

> I haven't been to any training where they say, 'This is for EAL children'. (F3)

> There hasn't really been anything specific for schools like this. (F3)

> [I haven't had] that much [EAL training] really, but I've just started, and I'm sure they'll put me on courses and that kind of thing, but not so far. (F6)

> We [at the Service] make inputs into our local [higher education] institutions [about initial teacher training] but it's very much an ad hoc basis. (F7)

Requests of mainstream teachers and members of EMAS staff for additional EAL training in English grammar and linguistics:

> I feel that [our training] should become more specialized and go more into the fields like linguistics so that you can more accurately describe the children's level of acquisition. (F1)

In the structure and vocabulary of pupils' first languages:

> Learning Arabic is something I'd really like to do ... [I worked with] Arabic parents last year, and I couldn't communicate with them at all ... It was so frustrating. (F3)

> [I would like to know] how their languages work because we push phonics and that kind of thing ... If I knew that, or other things in their language ... I could perhaps understand the misconceptions and spot them. (F6)

In pupils' cultural and religious backgrounds:

> And I think that somewhere down the line we need to talk about cultural issues and use of first language, and supporting these children culturally as well as academically. (F1)

In the role of community schools:

> I'm not sure where they go [when they leave for the mosques]. I'd like to know about that too. (F6)

(d) School leadership.

Involvement in community and government initiatives:

> So we're doing things that traditionally all-white middle class
> schools do; we're going to have a go at it. (F4)
> I think the school's involved in a lot of initiatives, like the
> Branson Project Initiative ... There are lots of projects going on
> ... they get involved in things like that. (F6)

(e) Professional relations and the status of EMAS staff.

Uncertainty regarding the role of EMAS staff:

> I find that you come in as a second-class person and have to
> prove yourself on an individual basis. And with children ...
> the teacher's at the front, with the marker pen, with the
> register ... it's her room, and she's got charge of all the
> important bits of the lesson, and you're going in just like in
> some schools a parent ... or a teaching assistant or a learning
> mentor [might] ... and so [pupils are] used to adults going in,
> but the perception is, 'That's the teacher. All the other adults
> are not teachers.' So then of course, with teachers, there's a
> psychological barrier to get through with them too. They don't
> see you as equal because you're not as busy as them ... It can
> be the worst thing in the job. It's this constant having to break
> through people's prejudices. (F1)

Mis-assignment of EMAS staff:

> People constantly want you to take the special needs children.
> (F1)

How a lack of time restricts the ability of EMAS staff and teachers to
undertake joint planning:

> But there's also the stress that people are under; they just have
> far too much to do, and far too much on their minds apart from
> just teaching, so that the last thing they want is to sit down
> with you for an hour and plan what they should be doing next
> week, if they know what they should be doing next week at
> that point. (F1)

> [You need more] time to sit down with the support staff that
> you're working with ... to get time before the lesson to discuss
> your role, their role, what you're doing this week. (F3)
> We often get [classroom assistants] taken out ... It's very hard
> to get some kind of pattern going when you work with
> somebody [who might be taken somewhere else]. (F3)

Inability of head teacher to *insist* that teachers and EMAS staff plan together:

> More time needs to be given, and ... that is a government priority, getting staff more non-contact time for planning ... [The government is] looking at that in next eighteen months, two years, where ... it's all to do with reducing burden, workload on teachers; there's a big push on that at the moment. And certainly one of the ways I feel I could use that is by saying right, well, you've got non-contact time, now I can then insist that EMAS staff work together with class teachers. At the moment, I'm on dodgy ground there because it's their own time, effectively. (F4)

Viability of planning and teaching in partnership, depending on the personalities of the teachers and instructors involved:

> Some people are easy to work with and some aren't. It's a very difficult one to get around. I mean I find that I support people on a personal level sometimes to get that rapport, or I gofer, you know, just at that initial stage until people feel comfortable with you. (F1)

> There are certain staff who just want an extra adult in the room and anybody will do, and then there are some people who genuinely use you properly, think about what they're doing, and everything works fine. (F1)

> It also depends on the person you're working with, because I know some of the support workers would rather sit at the back or just work with a few children because it's a confidence issue. (F3)

(f) Staffing allocations.

Shortage of EMAS/bilingual staff:

> [We need] more bilingual staff. I think every class should have a bilingual support assistant, a well-qualified bilingual support assistant, not necessarily qualified, but well-trained. (F4)

> So the key has got be to have as many bilingual staff as possible. Bilingual staff have still got to be good quality teachers and educators. (F4)

See also 'First-language development and literacy', above.

Pupils who are underachieving and/or who are preparing for SATs assessments as more likely to receive EMAS support than those with the lowest English-language abilities:

> We're trying a lot of new initiatives at the moment because the school is massively underachieving ... so I'm just trying everything. (F1)

> We're here to raise achievement, so basically we're aiming at that middle band of pupils who are underachieving. (F1)

See also 'Assessment of EAL pupils', above.
Resulting restrictions of support:

> [There is a] lack of accessibility [because of] timetables. If I want to be in all the literacy hours, that would be fine with one class, but if I also want to see literacy hours in another class, they overlap. (F1)

> [The bilingual instructors] have this induction program, where they show them around, they'll take them out and teach them some basic English, and then they'll go and support them in class. But there are so many [new arrivals], there's not enough of us to do it on a regular basis. Because anyone on induction is out of class, it's a tradeoff. (F1)

(g) Complexities of first-language use.

Fear that EAL pupils are becoming 'deficient' in both their first language and English:

> One of the things that we're very concerned [about] is that our many of our Urdu/Punjabi speakers, the largest language group we've got, they are losing their Urdu and their Punjabi ... They are becoming, if you like, deficient in two languages. And of course this is our bilingual staff telling us [and] they are quite upset by the fact that these children are not getting the level of Punjabi that they used to come to school with, which we could then work with, because once a child has a concept in a language it's transferable to another language. (F7)

Language hierarchies:

> The message we've got to get across is all languages ... do the same job. They are all high-functioning languages ... but our children have this ... hierarchy of languages. And even in the social context as well, the working people will just have their local languages. The [upper] classes will be able to speak in

Urdu, write and read in Urdu, and the upper echelons, even among their own company, will speak English. (F7)

APPENDIX I
Proposition 227

Proposition 227 was a state referendum in California which called for the abolition of bilingual education and the establishment of English-only instruction. The referendum passed on 2 June, 1998 with 61% in favour of the measure.

The following is an excerpt from the Statute, originally available online and now found in *At War with Diversity* (Crawford, 2000, p. 95):

(a) WHEREAS the English language is the national public language of the United States of America and the state of California, is spoken by the vast majority of California residents, and is also the leading world language for science, technology, and business, thereby being the language of economic opportunity; and

(b) WHEREAS immigrant parents are eager to have their children acquire a good knowledge of English, thereby allowing them to fully participate in the American Dream of economic and social advancement; and

(c) WHEREAS the government and the public schools of California have a moral obligation and a constitutional duty to provide all of California's children, regardless of their ethnicity or national origins, with the skills necessary to become productive members of our society, and of these skills, literacy in the English language is among the most important; and

(d) WHEREAS the public schools of California currently do a poor job of educating immigrant children, wasting financial resources on costly experimental language programs whose failure over the past two decades is demonstrated by the current high drop-out and low English literacy levels of many immigrant children; and

(e) WHEREAS young immigrant children can easily acquire full fluency in a new language, such as English, if they are heavily exposed to that language in the classroom at an early age.

(f) THEREFORE it is resolved that: all children in California public schools shall be taught English as rapidly and effectively as possible.

The statute prohibits most first-language instruction and prescribes programmes of 'sheltered English immersion during a temporary transition period not normally intended to exceed one year' (p. 96).

APPENDIX J
Texas' Elementary, Middle- and High-School Structure and Assessment System

In Texas and many other states, there is variation as to the grade levels included at each level of schooling. Options in Texas commonly include those shown in Figure A5 and Table AIII.

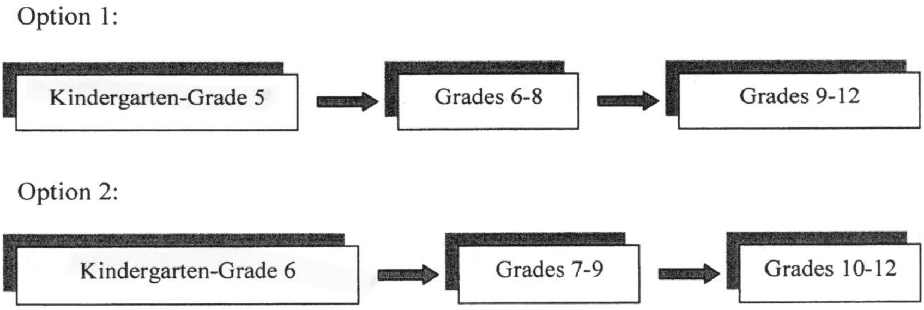

Option 1:

| Kindergarten-Grade 5 | → | Grades 6-8 | → | Grades 9-12 |

Option 2:

| Kindergarten-Grade 6 | → | Grades 7-9 | → | Grades 10-12 |

Figure A5. Options for Division of Schooling in Texas, by grade level.

Grade	Age
Kindergarten	5-6
1	6-7
2	7-8
3	8-9
4	9-10
5	10-11
6	11-12
7	12-13
8	13-14
9	14-15
10	15-16
11	16-17
12	17-18

Table AIII. Texas' school structure.

Students participate in the following annual state-wide assessments (TAKS):

Reading: grades 3 to 9
Writing: grades 4 to 7
English Language Arts: grades 10 and 11
Math: grades 3 to 11
Science: grades 5, 10, and 11
Social Studies: grades 8, 10, and 11

(Spanish versions are available for grades 3 to 6.)

For more information, see Texas Education Agency (2003).

APPENDIX K
The Four Blocks Literacy Framework

An explanation from Shady Ridge's school district website (accessed 30 March, 2003):

> The Four Blocks – Guided Reading, Self-Selected Reading, Writing, and Working with Words – represent four different approaches to teaching children to read. Daily instruction in all four blocks provides numerous and varied opportunities for all children to learn to read and write. Incorporating all four blocks acknowledges that children do not learn in the same way and provides substantial instruction to support whatever learning personality a child has.

An explanation from the school district's reading specialist (S15, e-mail communication, received 8 January, 2003):

> Four Blocks was adopted by [the district] in response to a request from our Superintendent to initiate a district-wide framework. We began with a first grade pilot group of about 35 teachers 5 years ago. We chose this framework for a variety of reasons. The balance of the blocks and the approach to phonics closely ties to our district reading philosophy. The writing block was also very important to our decision. We have enhanced the training by adding writing workshop training using the Fletcher text. We have gradually added each of the grades. This year we added fourth and fifth grades. This framework fits the needs of the variety of levels throughout our district. We have been to training in North Carolina several times and we have also sent several groups of teacher leaders to North Carolina to work with Patricia Cunningham and her

cohort of trainers. Most of the training in the district has been done by the six Literacy Specialists and a core of teacher leaders.

We have modified the guided reading block in the lower grades by implementing the Fountas and Pinnell model of small group guided reading. Some of our specialists have talked to Cheryl Sigmon and Pat Cunningham about this.

The bilingual training and support have been slowly added. Some of our specialists visited Four Blocks bilingual classrooms in New Mexico and we also sent a core of principals and teachers to New Mexico. This year we added a bilingual reading specialist at the district level. She was formally employed by ESC-20 and is very knowledgeable about Four Blocks. She has been a tremendous asset to our bilingual Four Blocks teachers. Our bilingual campuses have purchased leveled text in Spanish to use during Guided Reading. We also have established a Spanish benchmarking system to use with the Spanish program.

APPENDIX L
Reading Acceleration Program (RAP)

The RAP program is the district's form of accelerated reading instruction, mandated by the Texas Reading Initiative. Below is a description of the program at the state level, taken from the Texas Education Agency website (TEA, 2001).

Accelerated Reading Instruction

Accelerated Reading Instruction funding is given to each school district for early reading intervention on the basis of the number of students who did not pass the reading portion of TAAS at Grade 3 when the test was administered in the previous spring. This funding is to be used to provide intensive, targeted intervention programs for students at every campus students who have been identified as at-risk for reading difficulties, including dyslexia. Students are identified at Kindergarten, Grade 1 and Grade 2 using assessment instrument(s) on the Commissioner's Approved List of Early Reading Instruments called for under TEC Section §28.006. Early reading intervention through Accelerated Reading Instruction funding for the 2001-2002 school year must be used to address identified students in Kindergarten, Grade 1 and Grade 2.

APPENDIX M
Shady Ridge Elementary: interviewee information

- S1 is a first-grade bilingual teacher. He was born in Mexico, where he was educated as a chemical engineer and taught in a technical high school. After moving to the United States, he completed a university degree and obtained teacher certification. He has been teaching at Shady Ridge for three years and in the state for a total of nine years.

- S2 is a first-grade bilingual teacher. She grew up in the United States speaking Spanish as a first language, although she did not become fully biliterate until attending university. Before beginning her teaching career, she worked as an administrative assistant for a local business. She then enrolled at a local university to obtain her degree and teaching certificate, and after graduating began working at Shady Ridge. She has been teaching at Shady Ridge for nine years, the first four of which were at the fourth-grade level. Subsequently, she has been teaching first grade.

- S3 is a first-grade bilingual teacher. She grew up speaking both English and Spanish in a town along the Texas-Mexico border but believes that her Spanish skills have improved greatly since she began teaching. She completed her university training and teacher certification in 2001 and has worked at Shady Ridge as a first-grade teacher since then.

- S4 is a first-grade teacher of English as a second language (ESL). She completed her teacher training at a nearby university six years ago. This is her sixth year teaching and her fifth year as a first-grade teacher at Shady Ridge. She is a Spanish speaker and has also taught in the school's bilingual programme in the past.

- S5 is a fifth-grade ESL teacher. She is currently team-teaching with the bilingual fifth-grade teacher, S17. This is her third year teaching ESL at Shady Ridge.

- S6 is Shady Ridge's ESL specialist and has worked at the school for the last six years. Although born and educated in the United States, she lived in Mexico for eighteen years, after which she taught ESL in California. Currently, she divides her time between coordinating ESL and bilingual activities at the school and district level, as well as tutoring new ESL arrivals and teaching Spanish to native English speakers.

- S7 is a fourth-grade ESL teacher.

- S8 is the district's ESL/bilingual director. She has been working in the bilingual programme since 1978 and now coordinates district-level training and activities for the five elementary schools with ESL/bilingual programmes.

- S9 is a bilingual kindergarten teacher at Shady Ridge completing her seventh year teaching.
- S10 is a fourth-grade bilingual teacher.
- S11 is the principal at Shady Ridge. She taught at the elementary level for thirteen years before becoming a principal. After serving as a principal in two different schools in another state, she moved to Texas and has been Shady Ridge's principal for the last three years.
- S12 is a second-grade ESL teacher. She has also been a bilingual teacher at another school, but this is her first year teaching ESL.
- S13 is an ESL specialist at another cluster campus in the district.
- S14 is the ESOL (English for speakers of other languages) coordinator for the district. Her responsibilities include implementing ESL programmes district-wide for middle and high schools.
- S15 is a district-level Four Blocks specialist.
- S16 is a kindergarten bilingual teacher.
- S17 is the fifth-grade bilingual teacher who team-teaches with ESL teacher S5.

APPENDIX N
Shady Ridge Elementary: language demographics

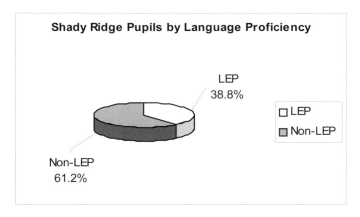

*Non-LEP pupils are either native English speakers or pupils who are considered fluent in English, according to oral or reading assessments.

Figure A6. Shady Ridge pupils by language proficiency (total pupils: 613).

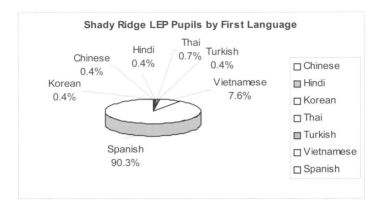

Figure A7. Shady Ridge LEP pupils by first language (total pupils: 278).

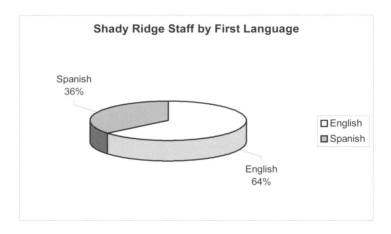

Figure A8. Shady Ridge staff by first language (total staff: 71).

APPENDIX O
Shady Ridge Elementary: ethnic demographics

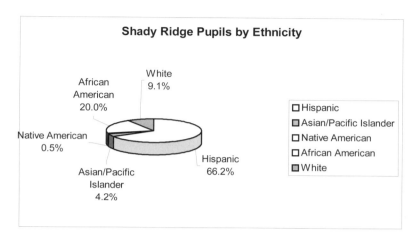

Figure A9. Shady Ridge pupils by ethnicity.

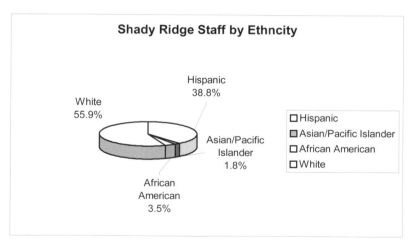

*This information has been included to account for the racial and ethnic diversity of the school that is not related to first languages.

Figure A10. Shady Ridge staff by ethnicity.

APPENDIX P
Extracts from Taped Interviews:
Shady Ridge Elementary and district staff

The following is a selection of the quotations referred to, but not included, in Chapter Six. In addition, more information has been gleaned from untaped interviews with teachers and staff at the school.

1. Pupil and Community Characteristics

Moderate stability of the LEP population at Shady Ridge and in the district:

> We don't get as many upper grade students coming in, [although] we do get some. (S8)

> [Except for one cluster school in the district] pretty much all the others are pretty stable [in their LEP populations]. (S8)

Differences between the ethos of the bilingual and ESL classrooms, with respect to bilingual pupils:

> Their social skills, as far [as] the respect they have for elders, for teachers ... I don't know why, but there's just a difference [in] the way the bilingual kids behave and follow rules versus the English kids. (S9)

> Mine just do [have pride] ... They watch telenovelas and they're proud of it, their grandma[s] make them tortillas and they're proud of it. (S10)

ESL pupils:

> I really feel embarrassed, because some of the kids I have here, they've got some behavior problems, and it takes me away from the main focus. I know some kids ... who really want to learn, but ... it's not fair. (S4)

> I can see the pride in their [bilingual] children ... You don't see the same pride [in ESL children]. (S7)

> How can you bring [ESL pupil performance] to be an average level? ... You can't. It's just so wide ... so everything is dumped into my classroom; it's how I feel sometimes. (S7)

> [With] the class that I have, one of the biggest struggles for me was discipline ... I've never done the ESL; I've always done bilingual and the bilingual kids are very well-behaved ... And

the ESL kids I have this year ... speak English very well, and they have been in the United States for a while, so they're very Americanized [and] they're very rowdy. (S12)

Parent participation in the school community:

Some are supportive, and some are not. (S2)

Those parents who are supportive you can count on your two hands. (S2)

I would [like to] have parents that are all very involved and would try to give me a little bit more support ... in these extra things that we do. (S3)

I invite the parents but a lot of them don't come because a lot of them work, both parents work. (S4)

[There's] not much ... parent involvement in our school, as much as I'd like there to be. (S4)

Parent satisfaction with the ESL/bilingual programme:

Over at other schools [parents want pupils exited] as soon as possible, but [not] here, because they know that when they come here, all the secretaries speak Spanish and ... the newsletters go home in Spanish. At other schools, there's not that attention. (S6)

The [ESL] parents like that they can ... have their little community, their Vietnamese community ... [The parents] aren't rushing to get them out, but if we, as teachers, decide to get them out, they take it as, 'We [the teachers] know better'. (S6)

2. Recent Reorganizations and Changes

Impact of staff 'reconstitution' in creating a more positive school environment:

We have a very *strong* bilingual team ... Coming from the old [Shady Ridge], I can tell you that really makes a difference when you have teachers that are proficient in the language, when you have teachers that are dedicated to their profession and especially very considerate about the needs of our students. (S2)

Before, out of eighteen [bilingual/ESL teachers], six to eight
would leave every year ... and last year [after the
reconstitution], nobody left, and so they're ... happy with [the
principal]. (S6)

Before ... this was a low-performing school, and now we're
doing everything we can to ... help make this school more
open ... more cheerful ... anything to help the kids learn better.
(S16)

Before [there] used to be ... a lot of arguing, a lot of
complaining in the hallways, and now it's just a lot more
cheerful and more of a family here now. (S16)

3. EAL/Bilingual Staff and Policy

Vague nature of the state's education code:

[The state education agency] is very good at giving up the law,
and then [nothing]. It's kind of like that site-based
management idea. (S14)

They give you a lot of rope [to hang yourself with] and I wish
they wouldn't. (S14)

Uncertainty regarding the implications of the *No Child Left Behind*
legislation:

[We have] all these thousands of pages of laws and right now
it's the interpretation time. So I haven't been giving all the
information to the teachers because we don't know what it is
yet. We don't know what tests they're going to be having in
April. (S6)

And what level of flexibility do we have? (S6)

It looks like [there will be stricter accountability] ... It's kind of
a step up. (S14)

There are some test instruments out there, but we don't know
what will be adopted yet ... and we're battling through that.
(S14)

The need for a coherent yet flexible district model for the bilingual
programme:

[We need] lots of flexibility, yes, because our ... cluster
campuses vary [in] the number of students, [and in] the socio-

economic status of some of the students ... and so yes, there's got to be a lot of flexibility. (S8)

Desired expansion of the ESL/bilingual programme:

I'd like to have a bilingual program at every campus and eliminate all our denials. (S8)

An ideal would be to have a program at your home campus so you don't have to be bussed to another school that's not in your neighborhood. (S8)

Benefits of Shady Ridge's late-exit programme:

I think honestly that it's been very successful, and it is the way we interpret the program ... because most of the teachers understand that our job is to build every year, a little more on the language. (S1)

I think [it is] very successful. We've seen a lot of growth in our students. (S2)

And I want them to continue to use [Spanish]. And the thing I like about [Shady Ridge] is the bilingual program continues to fifth grade, so I want them to be really strong in their first language. (S3)

We also want to do that [transition] at a real appropriate time, so we really don't believe that we should be transitioning kids until they've gotten through that fourth grade writing TAAS, and that they've gotten a really good basis in their first language ... and then they seem to make that transition so much easier. (S11)

(a) English language development and literacy.

Adequacy of Four Blocks for ESL pupils:

The Four Blocks, I think ... is designed as a frame; in other words, it's a balanced literacy ... they're getting those [skills] on a daily basis. (S4)

For me, I think it's very easy to use; however, there is no time throughout the day to devote to English grammar, which is something I find lacking. (S5)

English instruction for new arrivals:

> When we get new non-Spanish arrivals, they get extra help, but as you know the magic ingredient is time. I have the new arrivals for thirty minutes a day (when I am not at other campuses, special ed[ucation] meetings, covering classes) as well as an assistant takes them to another room and goes over vocabulary and play[s] games with them twenty to thirty minutes a day. (S6, e-mail communication, 24 February, 2003)

English instruction in the bilingual programme:

> Now I know for a fact that [English instruction isn't] being done the way [it] should but we're working on it, and teachers can say, 'Yes, yes, yes,' but what goes on in the classroom when we're not there? But still, our scores have been pretty good. (S6)

Fifth-grade ESL/bilingual teaming:

> Once the tests were over, we started combining our classes. We figured that worked very well. Last year at the end of the year ... we did everything in English. (S5)

> My students, some of them come back, and they tell me ... they're not having any problems [in English-medium classes] so I'm guessing that it helped them. (S17)

English instruction and teacher S4:

> It's basically the same thing [that I would do in a non-ESL class], but more of it, more of the visual, more of the chanting. (S4)

> A lot of the time is spent on explaining and illustrating what a certain word means, or an idea. (S4)

> [I use] a lot of visual, a lot of repetition, and then how one gives the instruction ... also makes a difference ... You have to repeat yourself, and then you have to simplify it ... for them, and then they'll catch on. (S4)

> Their writing needs are different because their vocabulary is not really up to par ... I do give them opportunities to write. (S4)

> I expect a lot from them in reading. (S4)

English use in first-grade bilingual classrooms:

> We are including, little by little, English, like ... counting the days, the seasons, and then holidays, and songs that are in English. At the beginning of the year [in January], I start putting [up] some signs with the names of the items we have in school. (S1)

> I use the English in social studies. I use the English when I give instructions like, 'go into the hallway', 'go into the bathroom', in music, in art, and I feel that that is the conversational English that they have to acquire to be able to function in the school ... but I also use it, if, for instance, they want to talk to me in English. When I'm ... teaching language arts or writing or math, I don't stop them from it. I'll let them do it. It's just a very natural way of processing from their first language to their second language, so ... if they need me to explain it, I'll use it, but their English is developed ... as naturally as I can. (S2)

> [I use English in science and social studies] because ... it's at the end of the day. I don't know where else to fit in this forty-five minutes [of English] ... In math, I do it more now ... because they've told us we have to use it more. (S3)

> If I'm teaching about ... weather, we'll say all those terms [in English]. [If] we do the water cycle, I will explain it and we will do it and we will create it and we will experiment with it in Spanish. And then, we will talk about it in English, maybe at the last part of the day. (S3)

(b) First-language development and literacy.

On first-language skills strengthening second-language development:

> I feel like [it] is important for me to build a real[ly] good foundation where they can use their native language, the first language. (S2)

> I really feel that it is extremely important that a child has a strong foundation in their native language ... because all those strategies will transfer to the second language. (S3)

> Well, based on research, the stronger the language is, they go into the second language [stronger] ... Here in the United

States the only way to get that strong language is to have the bilingual [program]. (S6)

If they have a strong, solid foundation in their native language, they're able to [transfer those skills to English]. (S7)

If their native language is so-so, they have nothing to pull from to jump into the English. (S10)

On pupils feeling more comfortable interacting in their first language:

It's ... overwhelming to hear everything in another language. (S3)

When they come in, they want to hear somebody speaking their language. It makes it more comfortable for them when they come in ... [An English-only class] is very scary and it might withdraw them from being ... productive in their years in school. (S16)

On the enrichment and improvement of first-language competence as valuable in its own right:

I see it as an asset, because instead of them being monolingual, they're going to be bilingual. (S9)

In my classroom, the goal is always just to enrich their native language as much as possible. (S10)

We have the same goals and same visions for them that we do for all the other kids in the building. So there isn't a difference there. They have the added bonus of making that transition into English. (S11)

First-language use in teacher S4's classroom:

In their native country, they have some kind of celebrations. We bring that into the classroom. (S4)

[Pupil-pupil interaction] is all [in] English. (S4)

Development of Four Blocks Spanish curriculum:

We never thought we would have to [present the curriculum to others] ... it was more like a survival. We were dumped in this program, and we had to make it good. (S1)

When we went to Four Blocks [training] for language arts, what we received ... was not what I wanted. There [were] a lot of holes, a lot of questions in my mind. I struggled with it for about three weeks when we came in to school ... They just kept on telling us, 'Just do it the way the books tells you to do it,' and it wasn't going well...and so I decided to sit down and start writing a teacher's guide for bilingual teachers for Four Blocks. And it got to be really a long process, so I got [teacher S1] involved in it, and [he] helped me with finding other resources. (S2)

First-language development in first-grade bilingual classrooms:

We try to develop ... the basic skills, the fundamental skills for language and solving problems in the language the kids know better. So we teach reading, math ... mainly in Spanish. And also, at the beginning of the year, we use Spanish for science and social studies. We incorporate all the ... new concepts for the kids in the language they can understand. (S1)

I've forced myself to make them learn those words [they only know in English] in Spanish too. (S1)

I use Spanish in the classroom basically to teach my reading, my writing, and my math because I feel like that is important for me to build a real[ly] good foundation where they can use their native language, the first language. And then I use social studies and science to develop their second language, but ... I use that after I've already taught the lesson in Spanish. I build the background information first in their first language. (S2)

Teacher S3:

I use Spanish in the class when I'm teaching them content ... science [and] social studies [are] all taught in Spanish because ... it's their native language and I feel that they would understand all these terms [better] ... I feel that they would better relate to and understand [it] if it's in their language. And of course, reading [is taught in Spanish], because it's their native language ... And writing [is in Spanish], because that's how they express themselves verbally, so of course, written [work], they're going to do ... in Spanish too. (S3)

Math is also taught in Spanish because ... they can ... relate to it more ... I want them to grasp these concepts in their native language. (S3)

(c) Assessment of ESL/bilingual pupils.

Teachers' criticism of the previous state assessment:

> The break in cultures [is obvious] ... our kids didn't know what [the prompt] was; they'd never had that experience. (S2)

> I think the Spanish test in fourth grade ... is a lot more difficult than it is in English. Vocabulary is probably at sixth-grade level [and] the writing prompts were awful ... It's gotten better from what I've heard ... It was like the playing field wasn't even. (S2)

> [The tests assume that everyone comes from] an average family. And these are not average families, especially at this school. (S7)

> The tests drive me crazy ... They always gear it toward the norm. Always. (S10)

> [The Spanish-language tests are] very awkward for them because a lot of that language is not used in their own countries ... some of those words are not something that we're accustomed to ... it doesn't transfer the same ... Even for me, I have a few problems understanding what they're trying to say. Some of these words I'm not used to using, and I grew up in a [Spanish-speaking] household in Mexico. (S17)

On the Reading Inventory for ESL pupils:

> The TPRI [Texas Primary Reading Inventory], I ... personally don't feel that it's appropriate for ESL kids because of the vocabulary. They haven't been exposed to ... a lot of that vocabulary. And the phonemic awareness, some of them may have ... and some of them don't ... I think they ought to modify it in some way, allow more visual[s], because ... if you had pictures, that would help. (S4)

On the Reading Inventory for bilingual pupils:

> This year they changed it, and they included a section which all of them failed, where I had to say ... each sound of the word and they had to guess what word it was ... Spanish is not like that, it's syllabic. (S3)

First-grade bilingual teachers' attitudes regarding standardized assessments:

> I'm not for a lot of testing ... When I sit them in front of me, and do a test one to one, they won't do as well as I know they could. (S1)

> I don't give [classroom] assessments. My philosophy is they're six years old, they're still developing. If I can see that they're understanding the concept, and if they can demonstrate that they're developing, or if they can do it for me ... that's mastery. (S2)

> In fourth grade it would be totally different, but in this stage right here I'm looking for growth ... Assessments to me are what I can observe and what the kids can tell me if I ask them a question. (S2)

> We have to give them so often, and even the running record, the benchmarks, [are] hard, but I guess that's a part of life, they're always going to have tests. (S3)

5. Factors Affecting Language-in-Education Policy Implementation

(a) School funding and institutional support.

Beliefs regarding the basis of language-in-education policies:

> I think that's what legislators do, they have an opinion about something without really having [a] fundamental knowledge basis about education, and so they make policies based on their personal experience, as opposed to based on research ... and what's good for kids. And then they have [a] political agenda that sort of also overlooks all those things. (S13)

Support district-wide for the ESL/bilingual programme:

> [Support for ESL/bilingual at each school] varies with different administrators. (S6)

> Yes, [the district does] support us, yes, they do fund ... above the state allocations, but, I don't know how I would say this, [there is] mild support. (S8)

Potential impact of the new bilingual reading specialist:

> I'm not sure yet what her responsibilities are yet, but I think she's being kept very busy in the district office instead of in the schools. (S2)

> [She] will go to the five cluster schools, but I've seen her here, like, three times ... and she's zooming and working and doing many things that then she sends to us. (S6)

Assistance provided by the ESL specialist:

> [She] is a great support. She provides us with information about the bilingual program ... she just gives us a lot of materials, and also when we have a conference to go [to], she goes with us, so she knows what we are exposed to, and she knows what we think. (S1)

> We take our gripes and our concerns to her, and ... she voices our concerns, and really tries to help us ... She also is very resourceful, especially in the web site[s], so whenever she finds something, she does that for us. (S2)

> She knows how I ... like to teach, so she knows that I would really like more literature books, so she lets me know that I can ... go get them ... She's very willing to go and get these ... materials that I need. (S3)

> [If the ESL specialist] says that we really need [resources], then [the principal] will approve it most of the time. (S3)
> She has given me a lot of support and insight on the different cultures. (S4)

> She will help [us] with translating ... She's got a lot of people asking her to do it too. (S5)

First-grade teachers' reliance on each other as sources for pedagogical ideas, curricular materials, and teaching strategies: see 5(c) below.

(b) School resources.

Funding of ESL/bilingual programme at Shady Ridge:

> That [state funding is spent] according to the principal. In this school, we have that freedom [to use it for the bilingual program]. (S1)

> It's really weird that in the five schools, you'd think our ... budgets for bilingual would be similar, right? This principal has been very generous what we get, like ten or twelve thousand [dollars] while other schools, it's like 250 dollars. (S6)

More time needed to make first-language resources:

> We struggle a lot with getting things prepared, getting it right, and ... you're talking about lots of time, lots of time. If you're really dedicated to the program, and you want to do a good job, you're talking about a lot of time in the classroom. (S2)

> I really think that one day we need ... a 'make and take' [session]. We [would] make the activities that we need ... The next day we could already use them ... [We should have] maybe one each semester. (S3)

> [We need more] time [and] a translator, somebody to help ... with that translating, just so that [we don't] have to worry about any of it. (S5)

> She's got so much ... translating to do, she's just packed with translating, and it takes up so much of her time and energy. (S5, about team-teacher S17)

> [Other ESL specialists] didn't want [me] to put [translating] down [in my job description], which is a major part of [my job], because they don't do it and they don't want their principals to know ... Yes, we take great pride at [Shady Ridge] on our translations ... If we're trying to show how great the program is, whatever goes home should be first class ... but that can be major time. (S6)

General scarcity of bilingual resources:

> We have [resources] too, but we have to look for [them]. (S1)

> Our teachers go out and get things. Those that have known how wonderful it is to grow up [in a Spanish-speaking country] having the real things, they look for it ... The better the teacher is, the more they get. (S6)

> [We gather resources] here, there, and everywhere. (S8)

Inequities in the provision of English- and Spanish-language curriculum materials:

> We modify everything we need to ... it's like doing our job twice. (S2)

> No matter how much they give you, resources or money, you still have to adapt it to Spanish. (S2)

They don't purchase the same amount of stuff for everybody. I see it, and the kids see it ... [English-medium classes get] baskets and baskets of all these different things, and this (pointing to a shelf) is our library. And those books ... are just what we've found here ... I have some really bad books there that the librarian was just going to discard, [but] she gave them to me. And they're written on, and [the pupils] notice that the books that they read are written on. And we've explained that you don't write on books or anything, you take care of them, and they show me, they're like, 'Look!' [and I have to say], 'Sorry, that's what I have to give you to read'. (S3)

It's just not equitable. It never has been. (S8)

Probably the biggest challenge has just become the equity issue ... because the materials out there for our bilingual classrooms are scarce. (S11)

Availability of Spanish and other books for minority language pupils:

I would like to have ... a huge library, so the kids can be around all the books they [want] to read. And that is something that we don't have. It's better now than it was before; it's something [we've] been fighting for. We have more books, [and] we always wanted more books. (S1)

Our principal was real[ly] good. She has really developed a nice book room where we have enough Spanish literature to teach reading, where last year we didn't have anything. (S2)

Our library here is inadequate for bilingual education kids ... We don't have enough [reading books], so I have to go outside to get that. (S2)

They need to have more ... emergent literacy books ... They have a few, but not at [ESL pupils'] level. That would be great if they had those kinds of books. (S4)

Usefulness of district-adopted textbooks available in Spanish versions:

The textbooks – the reading is ridiculously hard, but it's ridiculously hard for our regular ed[ucation] kids. It's so far over their heads ... it's just not useable at all [without modifications]. They just take up space. (S5)

(c) Professional development and teacher training.

Principal's approach to teacher training:

> She ... really pushes for [ESL/bilingual teachers] to go to ... in-services. We haven't this year because it hasn't come ... up this much. The first two years we were here she sent them to everything [available] and last year I arranged probably six or seven times for people to go [to training sessions] and one day, every single [LEP] teacher and every single [LEP] assistant were out. The rest of the school didn't like it because the cafeteria went crazy, but she will allow things like that ... so she is very free with that [where] other principals aren't. (S6)

> We have a pretty clear picture of where we want to go; we don't do a lot of one day here, one day there, it's a lot of sustained staff development. (S11)

Variable responses to ESL/bilingual teacher training:

> [Even those sessions focused on bilingual pupils] didn't make any sense. We argued our points about how we taught reading, and we made our point. (S2)

> They convey a lot of research-based techniques and strategies, and we go to a lot of in-services that discuss things [and provide] materials that can be used for ESL kids and bilingual kids. (S4)

Value of building relationships training:

> When we started the year ... we started having some difficulties ... [With this training] we meet and we have some 'group therapy,' and it was excellent, I think, because [we were] very open, and we shared our views and our hopes, and after that, the rest of the year was getting better. (S1)

> One thing [the principal] says over and over [is], 'relationships and building relationships' ... Part of [our success] is the staff who [were] chosen, and part of it is strengthening the program. (S6)

> The other trainings as far as communicating with individuals and how to teach us to have a better environment [were helpful] ... because if you're having issues as teachers or with your principal ... then that gets brought into your classroom. (S9)

First-grade ESL and bilingual teachers' requests for additional training:

I would like to have writing training ... [I didn't go to one before] because I was kind of afraid because my English was not ... good. (S1)

[Successful training would be] something that's produced by teachers that are very aware of the grammar and the uses of Spanish, and are aware of the reading strategies that we need. (S2)

I would like to have [training on] how to use more literature in the classroom, and guided reading ... and ... how I should be teaching reading. (S3)

It would be very helpful to me as a teacher to understand more about [ESL pupils'] cultures ... and maybe learn a little bit of the language[s] ... to be able to communicate better with them. (S4)

What I would like is to have more training [in] effective teaching for ESL students, and [bringing] more success to them. (S4)

Value of teacher collaboration:

Teachers need to get together and talk about what's working, what's not working, and develop a manual. That's kind of like what we did [here] and it's been successful, but we've only kinda touched the little tip of the iceberg. We've got a long ways to go. (S2)

It really helped me to hear other teacher's ideas on what they did, at conferences, and even at our meetings here, like with [teachers S1 and S2], going to them and [asking], 'What do you?' and 'How [do you do it]?' ... I just try it out and see how it is, and if it works for me, then I'll continue doing [it]. (S3)

The teachers here, they share a lot of ideas ... There's some, [but] not a lot of communication, but I feel that it's a really close group when we do get together as a bilingual team. I just feel I have extra support. (S3)

Sometimes I go to [teacher S2]. She has some good ideas on teaching strategies for bilingual kids, and I kind of adapt it to my kids. (S4)

(d) School leadership.

The principal as a significant advocate for the ESL/bilingual programme:

> I really love that principal. She allows you to be creative and do what you can to make those connections with those kids. (S4)

> And recently we were concerned about whether [our team teaching] was working or not; we weren't sure, we had some doubts. We went and talked to [the principal] and she gave us a little pep talk and told us we were doing great and made us feel good about ourselves ... she just came in and checked in, and I think that helped. (S5)

> Principals don't want certain populations there, but our principal is a specialist in students who are at-risk. (S6)
> We also have an awesome principal. This is the second school I've taught in, and it's a difference of night and day ... She's so innovative, getting us so much training ... to show us the big picture. (S9)

The principal's perception of her contribution to bilingual teachers' support:

> They have smaller class sizes than everybody else does. For the most part, they all have an assistant that at least comes into their room for part of the week ... [I] also allocate ... a good portion of our budget ... towards just their ... Spanish materials. (S11)

Lack of state assessment pressure from school leadership:

> Not with this principal, but with other principals ... [testing pressure] makes your life miserable. (S6)

> I am not a test focused principal, I can tell you that right now ... It is a measurement of how we're doing though. (S11)

> So, the test is not my focus. However ... assessment is also important because it should be driving where we're going and what we're doing, and the goal is really just to create a literature-rich environment and taking science and social studies and integrating it into everything that we're doing during the day, so that's our focus. That test is just the byproduct of what we do as far as I'm concerned...We're going to focus on giving good quality instruction. If we're teaching to the standards, and we're giving good quality instruction, really

the only thing you need to teach the kids is the format of the test. (S11)

(e) Professional relations and the status of ESL/bilingual staff.

General equality among staff:

There's something special about [Shady Ridge] …. There can be different things going on … between the [teachers in the ESL/bilingual] program and those that [teach native speakers of] English, and different subtleties, but I think all in all, it's okay. (S6)

Professional disadvantage when material resources are provided exclusively for English-medium teachers:

In English, they already had these books developed by other people … and so all they had to do was open up the book … well we didn't have that. (S2)

We have to make up everything … other teachers get them … and we [don't] … We have to do it all. (S3)

(f) Staffing allocations.

Staff responsiveness to ESL/bilingual pupils' needs:

We're lucky at our school [to have good bilingual staff] …. [It's because] of the luck of the draw of who you have, but part of it … is the way [the principal] interviews. She has an intuitiveness and she knows within a few seconds if the person will fit in or not. (S6)

When our families walk in … there is somebody in this building … for them to be able to converse with, whether they're English or Spanish speaking. (S11)

Allocation of more skilled bilingual teachers to the lower grades:

We would put the best [bilingual] teachers in 3rd, 4th, and 5th to pass the TAAS [but now we put] good teachers down at the bottom [grades], and now the 3rd, 4th, and 5th [grade teachers] see that [the pupils] can do the test. (S6)

Allocation of assistants:

According to the … state, all the bilingual program teachers have a stipend, because of all the extra work that we do. In this school district, the stipend is gone, and then they hire us, saying that, 'We don't give you the stipend because you [are going to] have an assistant all the time', which is not true ... I would like to have an assistant because that [allows] me to do more of my teaching. (S1)

When ... I interviewed here, the woman in charge of personnel said, 'Come to my school district. We don't have a stipend [for bilingual teachers], but your class will never be over 15 and you have a full-time assistant' ... So there were eighteen bilingual teachers and eighteen assistants [at Shady Ridge]. That lasted one year. Now there are eighteen [teachers], and we have five and a half [assistants]. (S6)

Preferences varied for all-LEP ESL classes or mixed LEP/non-LEP classes. Some of the ESL teachers would prefer a 'true' ESL class:

[I would prefer] not to have everything dumped into one class. (S7)

Other ESL teachers find that there is little difference between teaching 'mixed' or all-ESL classes:

I don't think it's much different ... The two students [I had last year] that were not ESL ... were very immature, and I had to use the same strategies for them. (S4)

(g) Complexities of first-language use.

Some bilingual teachers' beliefs that their Spanish literacy skills were underdeveloped before teaching:

I grew up speaking Spanish. I grew up in a border town ... I spoke English more [than Spanish]...in school, and at home, it'd be both; my parents speak both, and it was very mixed. It's 'Spanglish,' and it was bad. Whatever word you didn't know in Spanish, you could just say it in English and everybody would understand you. (S3)

I realized how bad my vocabulary in Spanish was when I had to sit down with these kids and actually carry on a whole conversation in Spanish, everything in Spanish. (S3)

I didn't have to go around writing with accent [marks] and all that ... I didn't have any place where I had to put it into practice ... until here. (S9)

My first year of teaching was difficult; the kids knew more Spanish than I did. They helped me out a lot that first year. (S16)

Complexities of translation:

> People just have this misconception that you can translate completely [from] English into Spanish. (S2)

> For science, I'm not sure of half of the words on there [in Spanish]. I have to look them up and make sure I have the correct word or the one they use in the book, or the one they use in the TEKS ... When [the ESL specialist translates], she has to send it to me and tells me to look over it, see if the words are correct, or if [I] want to replace it with something. (S17)

> Translating a lot of stuff is very hectic. And I don't know if I'm translating well enough to where they'll be able to use those skills for their testing. (S17)

Variations in pupils' relative strengths in English and Spanish:

> It varies from year to year. I don't know if that depends on the teacher they had in kinder, or the time they spend watching TV, because ... last year, the kids that came from kinder ... they were not using a lot of English. This year, I have a lot of kids that are more fluent in English somehow, not really proficient, not yet, but they can understand more. (S1)
> It's like every class is different, every class has different needs, every year. (S2)

Pupils' Spanish vocabularies:

> If the family at home ... have some level of education ... from their own country ... they tend to use the Spanish more properly ... and if the family is ... a working level family, the level of the Spanish they use is very poor, so they rely a lot on English, because the families at home use a very limited vocabulary, so they don't have much background. (S1)

Differences between academic Spanish and that spoken in the home:

> I have to be attentive ... because sometimes the language that I use is not the language they understand. (S1)

> Everybody has different vocabulary, you know, certain words are different, so some of the words I was taught ... was not [what they were saying]. (S16)

Bibliography

Academic Excellence Indicator System (AEIS) (2002) Selected AEIS Campus Data: a multi-year history. Available at: www.tea.state.tx.us

Ager, D. (1996) *Language Policies in Britain and France: the processes of policy.* London: Cassell.

Ager, D. (2001) *Motivation in Language Planning and Language Policy.* Clevedon: Multilingual Matters.

August, D. & Hakuta, K. (1997) *Improving Schooling for Language Minority Children: a research agenda.* Washington, DC: National Academy Press.

Baker, C. & Jones, S.P. (1998) *Encyclopedia of Bilingualism and Bilingual Education.* Clevedon: Multilingual Matters.

Bassey, M. (1999) *Case Study Research in Educational Settings.* Buckingham: Open University Press.

Bereday, G.Z. (1964) *Comparative Method in Education.* New York: Holt, Rinehart & Wilson.

Berman, P. et al (1995) *School Reform and Student Diversity: case studies of exemplary practices for LEP students.* Santa Cruz: National Center for Research on Cultural Diversity and Second Language Learning.

Biggs, A.P. & Edwards, V. (1991) 'I Treat Them All the Same': teacher-pupil talk in multi-ethnic classrooms, *Language and Education,* 5(3), pp. 161-176.

Bray, M. & Thomas, R.M. (1995) Levels of Comparison in Educational Studies: different insights from different literatures and the value of multilevel analyses, *Harvard Educational Review,* 65(3), pp. 472-490.

Brumfit, C. (1995) *Language Education in the National Curriculum.* Oxford: Blackwell.

Cable, C. & Leung, C. (1997) *English as an Additional Language: changing perspectives.* Watford: National Association for Language Development in the Curriculum.

Cardinale, K., Carnoy, M. & Stein, S. (1999) Bilingual Education for Limited English Proficiency Students: local interests and resource availability as determinants of pedagogical practice, *Qualitative Studies in Education,* 12(1), pp. 37-57.

Carrasquillo, A.L. & Rodriguez, V. (2001) *Language Minority Students in the Mainstream Classroom.* Clevedon: Multilingual Matters.

Cobarrubias, J. (1983) Ethical Issues in Status Planning, in J. Cobarrubias & J. Fishman (Eds) *Progress in Language Planning: international perspectives.* Berlin: Mouton de Gruyter.

Cohen, L., Manion, L. & Morrison, K. (2000) *Research Methods in Education*, 5th ed. London: RoutledgeFalmer.

Committee of Inquiry into the Education of Children from Ethnic Minority Groups (1985) *Education for All: the report of the Committee of Inquiry into the Education of Children from Ethnic Minority Groups (Swann Report).* London: HMSO.

Committee of Inquiry into the Teaching of English Language (1988) *Report of the Committee of Inquiry into the Teaching of English Language: appointed by the Secretary of State under the chairmanship of Sir John Kingman.* London: HMSO.

Cooper, R.L. (1989) *Language Planning and Social Change.* Cambridge: Cambridge University Press.

Corson, D. (1990) *Language Policy across the Curriculum.* Clevedon: Multilingual Matters.

Corson, D. (1991) Realities of Teaching in a Multiethnic School, *International Review of Education*, 37(1), pp. 7-32.

Corson, D. (1998) *Changing Education for Diversity.* Buckingham: Open University Press.

Coulmas, F. (1998) Language Rights: interests of state, language groups and the individual, *Language Sciences*, 20(1), pp. 63-72.

Crawford, J. (2000) *At War with Diversity: US language policy in an age of anxiety.* Clevedon: Multilingual Matters.

Crawford, J. (2002) Obituary: the Bilingual Ed Act, 1968-2002. Available at: http://www.rethinkingschools.org/special_reports/bilingual/Bil164.shtml

Cummins, J. (2001a) The Role and Use of Educational Theory in Formulating Language Policy, in C. Baker & N.H. Hornberger (Eds) *An Introductory Reader to the Writings of Jim Cummins.* Clevedon: Multilingual Matters.

Cummins, J. (2001b) Multicultural Education and Technology, in C. Baker & N.H. Hornberger (Eds) *An Introductory Reader to the Writings of Jim Cummins.* Clevedon: Multilingual Matters.

Cummins, J. & Swain, M. (1986) *Bilingualism in Education.* London: Longman.

De Beaugrande, R. (1999) Theory and Practice in the Discourse of Language Planning, *World Englishes*, 18(2), pp. 107-121.

Department for Education and Employment (DfEE) (1998a) *The Management of Literacy at School Level.* London: HMSO.

Department for Education and Employment (DfEE) (1998b) *The National Literacy Strategy: framework for teaching.* London: HMSO.

Department for Education and Employment (DfEE) (1998c) Ethnic Minority Achievement Grant: objectives. Available at: http://www.dfee.gov.uk/ethnic/supment.htm

Department for Education and Employment (DfEE) (1999a) *Statistical First Release: minority ethnic pupils in maintained schools by local education authority areas in England – January 1999 (provisional)*. London: Government Statistical Service.

Department for Education and Employment (DfEE) (1999b) *English: the National Curriculum for England (program of study)*. London: HMSO.

Department for Education and Skills (DfES) (2000) The National Literacy Strategy. Available at: http://www.standards.dfes.gov.uk/literacy/about/?a=fwa&art_id=81

Department for Education and Skills (DfES) (2002) *The National Literacy Strategy: supporting pupils learning English as an additional language*. London: HMSO.

Department for Education and Skills (DfES) (2003a) Ethnic Minority Achievement Grant. Available at: http://www.standards.dfes.gov.uk/ethnicminorities/raising_achievement/?template=C&art_id=490

Department for Education and Skills (DfES) (2003b) The Parents' Centre: curriculum and assessment. Available at: http://www.dfes.gov.uk/parents/curriculum/home.cfm

Department of Education and Science (DES) (1975) *A Language for Life (Bullock Report)*. London: HMSO.

Department of Education and Science (DES) (1989) *English for Ages 5 to 16 (Cox Report)*. London: HMSO.

Fishman, J. (1972) *The Sociology of Language: an interdisciplinary social sciences approach to language in society*. Rowley: Newbury House.

Fuhrmann, J. (2003) *Four Blocks Literacy Framework*. Available at: www.blocks4reading.com/fourblocks

Gillham, B. (2000) *Case Study Research Methods*. London: Continuum.

Gravelle, M. (1996) Supporting Bilingual Learners in Schools. Stoke-on-Trent: Trentham Books.

Hall, D. (1995) *Assessing the Needs of Bilingual Pupils: living in two languages*. London: David Fulton.

Hall, S. (1988) New Ethnicities, in A. Rattansi & J. Donald (Eds) '*Race', Cultures and Difference*. London: Sage/Open University.

Haque, Z. & Bell, J. (2001) Evaluating the Performance of Minority Ethnic Pupils in the Secondary Schools, *Oxford Review of Education*, 27(3), pp. 357-368.

Harris, R. (1997) Romantic Bilingualism: time for a change?, in C. Cable & C. Leung (Eds) *English as an Additional Language: changing perspectives*. Watford: National Association for Language Development in the Curriculum.

Herriman, M. & Burnaby, B. (1996) Introduction, in M. Herriman & B. Burnaby (Eds) *Language Policies in English-Dominant Countries: six case studies*. Clevedon: Multilingual Matters.

Hirsch, E.D. (1988) *Cultural Literacy: what every American needs to know*. New York: Vintage.

Holdaway, E.A. (1991) Recent Developments in Education in Britain: issues and implications, *International Journal of Educational Management*, 5(1), pp. 13-22.

Hornberger, N. (1994) Literacy and Language Planning, *Language and Education*, 8(1-2), pp. 75-86.

Horvath, B. (1980) *The Education of Migrant Children: a language planning perspective*. ERDC Report no. 24. Canberra: Australian Government Publishing Service.

Jones, P. (1971) *Comparative Education: purpose and method*. St Lucia: University of Queensland Press.

Kaplan, R.B. & Baldauf, Jr., R.B. (1997) *Language Planning from Practice to Theory*. Clevedon: Multilingual Matters.

Kindler, A. (2002) *Survey of the States' Limited English Proficient Students and Available Educational Programs and Services: 1999-2000 summary report*. Washington, DC: National Clearinghouse for English Language Acquisition and Language Instruction Educational Programs.

King, E.J. (1966) *Education and Social Change*. Oxford: Pergamon.

Kitwood, T.M. (1977) Values in Adolescent Life: towards a critical description. Unpublished Ph.D. dissertation, School of Education, University of Bradford.

Kloss, H. (1971) The Language Rights of Immigrant Groups, *International Migration Review*, 5, pp. 250-268.

Leung, C. (2001) England: ESL in the early days, in B. Mohan, C. Leung & C. Davison (Eds) *English as a Second Language in the Mainstream*. Harlow: Pearson.

Leung, C., Harris, R. & Rampton, B. (1997) The Idealised Native Speaker, Reified Ethnicities, and Classroom Realities, *TESOL Quarterly*, 31(3), pp. 543-560.

Lindholm-Leary, K.J. (2001) *Dual Language Education*. Clevedon: Multilingual Matters.

May, S. (2001) *Language and Minority Rights: ethnicity, nationalism and the politics of language*. Harlow: Pearson.

McLaughlin, B. (1992) *Myths and Misconceptions about Second Language Learning: what every teacher needs to unlearn*. Educational Practice Report No. 5. Santa Cruz: National Center for Research on Cultural Diversity and Second Language Learning.

Miedema, W. (1997) Linguistic Diversity and Education for Democracy in a Multicultural Society, *European Journal of Intercultural Studies*, 8(1), pp. 53-61.

Mohan, B., Leung, C. & Davison, C. (2001) Conclusion, in B. Mohan, C. Leung & C. Davison (Eds) *English as a Second Language in the Mainstream*. Harlow: Pearson.

National Association for Language Development in the Curriculum (NALDIC) (1998) *Provision in Literacy Hours for Pupils Learning English as an Additional Language*. Watford: National Association for Language Development in the Curriculum.

National Center for Educational Statistics (NCES) (2002) Core of Common Data, 1998-99 through 2001-02. Available at: http://www.ncela.gwu.edu/states/stateposter.pdf

National Clearinghouse for English Language Acquisition (NCELA) (1999) Which States Have Legislative Provisions for Limited English Proficient Student Instructional Programs? Available at: www.ncela.gwu.edu/askncela/18instruction.htm

National Clearinghouse for English Language Acquisition (NCELA) (2002a) How Has Federal Policy for Language Minority Students Evolved in the US? Available at: www.ncela.gwu.edu/askncela/03history.htm

National Clearinghouse for English Language Acquisition (NCELA) (2002b) The National Clearinghouse for English Language Acquisition & Language Instruction Educational Programs: about NCELA. Available at: http://www.ncela.gwu.edu/about.htm

National Clearinghouse for English Language Acquisition (NCELA) (2002c) Which States Offer Certification or Endorsement in Bilingual Education or ESL. Available at: www.ncela.gwu.edu/askncela/09certif.htm

Nisbet, J. & Watt, J. (1984) Case Study, in J. Bell, T. Bush, A. Fox, J. Goodley & S. Goulding (Eds) *Conducting Small-Scale Investigations in Educational Management*. London: Harper & Row.

Noah, H. (1986) The Use and Abuse of Comparative Education, in P.C. Altbach & G.P. Kelly (Eds) *New Approaches to Comparative Education*. London: University of Chicago Press.

Northern Association of Support Services for Equality and Achievement (NASSEA) (2001) *EAL Assessment: guidance on the NASSEA EAL assessment system*. Dukinfield: NASSEA.

Nyakatawa, S. & Siraj-Blatchford, I. (1994) Bilingualism, Biculturalism and Learning in Early Years Classrooms, in A. Blackledge (Ed.) *Teaching Bilingual Children*. Stoke-on-Trent: Trentham Books.

Office for Standards in Education (OFSTED) (1999) *Raising the Attainment of Minority Ethnic Pupils: school and LEA responses*. London: HMSO.

Office for Standards in Education (OFSTED) (2001a) *PANDA report for ____ primary school*. London: HMSO.

Office for Standards in Education (OFSTED) (2001b) *Managing Support for the Attainment of Pupils from Minority Ethnic Groups*. London: OFSTED.

Office for Standards in Education (OFSTED) (2002) *The National Literacy Strategy: the first four years 1998-2002*. London: HMSO.

Patton, M.G. (1980) *Qualitative Evaluation Methods*. Beverly Hills: Sage.

Paulston, C.B. (1990) Educational Policies in Utopia, in B. Harley, P. Allen, J. Cummins & M. Swain (Eds) *The Development of Second Language Proficiency*. Cambridge: Cambridge University Press.

Phillips, D. (1999) On Comparing, in R. Alexander, P. Broadfoot & D. Phillips (Eds) *Learning from Comparing: contexts, classrooms and outcomes*. Wallingford: Symposium Books.

Phillipson, R. (1992) *Linguistic Imperialism*. Oxford: Oxford University Press.

Putney, L.G. & Wink, J. (1998) Breaking the Rules: constructing avenues of access in multilingual classrooms, *TESOL Quarterly*, 7(3), pp. 29-34.

Qualifications and Curriculum Authority (QCA) (1999) *The National Curriculum: handbook for primary teachers in England*. London: HMSO.

Qualifications and Curriculum Authority (QCA) (2000) *A Language in Common: assessing English as an additional language*. London: HMSO.

Ramirez, J.D., Yuen, S.D., Ramey, D.R., Pasta, D.J. & Billings, D.K. (1991) *Final Report: longitudinal study of structural English immersion strategy, early-exit, and late-exit transitional bilingual education programs for language-minority children*. Executive summary. San Mateo: Aguirre International.

Rampton, B. (1990) Displacing the 'Native Speaker': expertise, affiliation and inheritance, *ELT Journal*, 44, pp. 97-104.

Rassool, N. (1995) Language, Cultural Pluralism and the Silencing of Minority Discourses in England and Wales, *Journal of Educational Policy*, 10(3), pp. 287-302.

Ricento, T. (1996) Language Policy in the United States, in M. Herriman & B. Burnaby (Eds) *Language Policies in English-Dominant Countries: six case studies*. Clevedon: Multilingual Matters.

Ricento, T. (2000) Historical and Theoretical Perspectives in Language Policy and Planning, in T. Ricento (Ed.) *Ideology, Politics and Language Policies – focus on English*, pp. 9-24. Amsterdam: Benjamins.

Rubin, J. (1977) Bilingual Education and Language Planning, in B. Spolsky & R.L. Cooper (Eds) *Frontiers of Bilingual Education*. Rowley: Newbury House.

Ruiz, R. (1990) Official Languages and Language Planning, in K. Adams & D. Brinks (Eds) *Perspectives on Official English: the campaign for English as the official language of the USA*. Berlin: Mouton de Gruyter.

San Miguel, Jr., G. (1987) *'Let All of Them Take Heed': Mexican Americans and the campaign for educational equality in Texas, 1910-1981*. Austin: University of Texas Press.

Schmidt, R. (2000) *Language Policy and Identity Politics in the United States*. Philadelphia: Temple University Press.

Snow, C.E., Burns, M.S. & Griffin, P. (1998) *Preventing Learning Difficulties in Young Children*. Washington, DC: National Academy Press.

Stake, R.E. (1994) Case Studies, in N.K. Denzin & S. Lincoln (Eds) *Handbook of Qualitative Research*. London: Sage.

Stubbs, M. (1991) Educational Language Planning in England and Wales: multicultural rhetoric and assimilationist assumptions, in F. Coulmas (Ed.) *A Language Policy for the European Community: prospects and quandaries*. Berlin: Mouton de Gruyter.

Swann, M.M. (1985) *Education for All: a brief guide to the main issues of the report*. London: HMSO.

Teacher Training Agency (TTA) (2000) *Raising the Attainment of Minority Ethnic Pupils*. London: Teacher Training Agency.

Teachers of English to Speakers of Other Languages (TESOL) (1997) ESL Standards for Pre-K-12 students. Available at: http://www.tesol.org/assoc/k12standards/it/01.html

Texas Administrative Code (TAC) (1998) *Title 19, Part II, Chapter 128. Texas Essential Knowledge and Skills for Spanish Language Arts and English as a Second Language.*

Texas Administrative Code (TAC) (2001) *Title 19, Part II, Chapter 101. Subchapter AA. Commissioner's Rules Concerning the Participation of Limited English Proficient Students in State Assessments.*

Texas Administrative Code (TAC) (2002) *Title 19, Part II, Chapter 89. Subchapter BB. Commissioner's Rules Concerning State Plan for Educating Limited English Proficient Students.*

Texas Education Agency (TEA) (1998) *Policy Research Report #10: academic achievement of elementary students with limited English proficiency in Texas public schools.* Document number GE8-600-03. Austin: Texas Education Agency.

Texas Education Agency (TEA) (2001) Texas Reading Initiative. Available at: http://www.tea.state.tx.us/reading/interest/accreains.html

Texas Education Agency (TEA) (2003) Assessment/Testing. Available at: http://www.tea.state.tx.us/assessment.html

Texas Education Agency Program Evaluation Unit (2000) *Texas Successful Schools Study: quality education for limited English proficient students.* Austin: Texas Education Agency.

Texas Education Code (TEC) (1995) *Title 2, Chapter 29. Subchapter B. Bilingual Education and Special Language Programs.*

Theisen, G. & Adams, D. (1990) Comparative Education Research, in R.M. Thomas (Ed.) *International Comparative Education: practice, issues, and prospects.* Oxford: Butterworth-Heinemann.

Thomas, W.P. & Collier, V.P. (1997) *School Effectiveness for Language Minority Students.* Washington, DC: National Clearinghouse of Bilingual Education.

Thomas, W.P. & Collier, V.P. (2001) A National Study of School Effectiveness for Language Minority Students' Long-Term Academic Achievement. Center for Research on Education, Diversity and Excellence. Available at: http://www.crede.uscs.edu/research/llaa/1.1_final.html

Thompson, L., Fleming, M. & Byram, M. (1996) Language Policy in Britain, in M. Herriman & B. Burnaby (Eds) *Language Policies in English-Dominant Countries: six case studies.* Clevedon: Multilingual Matters.

United States Census Bureau (2000) Census 2000 Redistributing Data Summary File. Available at: http://factfinder.census.gov

United States Department of Education (2001) No Child Left Behind: Title III – language instruction for limited English proficient and immigrant students. Available at: http://www.ed.gov/legislation/ESEA02/pg38.html

Vulliamy, G., Lewin, K. & Stephens, D. (1990) *Doing Educational Research in Developing Countries.* Basingstoke: Falmer Press.

Walford, G. (2001) *Doing Qualitative Educational Research: a personal guide to the research process.* London: Continuum.

Wertheimer, C. & Honingsfeld, A. (2000) Preparing ESL Students to Meet the New Requirements, *TESOL Journal*, 9(1), pp. 23-28.

Wiley, T.G. (2000) Continuity and Change in the Function of Language Ideologies in the United States, in T. Ricento (Ed.) *Ideology, Politics, and Language Policies: focus on English.* Amsterdam: Benjamins.

Yin, R.K. (1994) *Case Study Research: design and methods,* 2nd ed. London: Sage.